Glimpses of Notes

an autobiography

Alan Corkish

The author and erbacce-press would like to say a very special thank you to Walter Wanat and his team at booksfactory whose amazing new laser technology has made this book possible:

www.booksfactory.co.uk

Published in Liverpool UK by erbacce-press 2013.

Cover design and typesetting: Alan Corkish

First and limited edition of 50; signed and numbered

37/50

erbacce-press Liverpool UK
ISBN: 978-1-907878-60-2

Index:

Critical Commentary:

Luis Benítez: (Argentinian poet and writer; Compagnon de la Poésie)

Set in the landscape of the new British poetry, this work startles the reader with its strong passion for words and its concise construction of verses and pauses. With this autobiographical poem, Corkish (a poet I have long admired) confirms not only his talent, but also his skill and mastery of technique for to make poetry with his life, and to infuse life into every verse of this long work is sheer artistry. A work to read and re-read and the more I read it the more I like it! Really, a masterpiece! As both a reader and a poet, I say: 'I want to have lived this life, I want to have written this magnificent poem.'

Idris Caffrey: (Welsh poet)

Few poets would be brave enough to attempt what Alan Corkish has done in *Glimpses of Notes*,an autobiography in a very different format to what readers will be used to. Touching, warm, intelligent, humorous and yet critical and opinionated. It hooked me completely. I found the book impossible to put down until I reached the end... and then I started to read it all over again.

Jean Hull Herman: (USA based writer; editor of both *Möbius* and *The Pen Woman*)

Alan Corkish's work embodies totally new techniques in a revolutionary new poetic form. He offers options. He crosses the borders that define auditory and visual poetry. The technology used to present information is never neutral: words leap as fast as thoughts. Alan's stance seems to shout at you that we still need poetry, even if it isn't in the 'populist' mode of the moment. I'm not anywhere near the margins of the page or the world. Everything old is new again - this 'telling' was good enough for the people in the beginning: how can any listener be surprised that hardwired auditory perception has survived? The tension between the language and the layout is refreshingly illuminating. A totally new and exciting poetry, a major innovative work of art.

Helen Kitson: (UK based award-winning poet and short story writer)

An autobiography in verse might sound like a grim, solipsistic affair. It is to Alan Corkish's credit that he has brought it off rather magnificently - with humour and an awareness of the world around him. Indeed, the footnotes explaining significant world events provide a context and framework - footnotes can be irritating, but in this poem they are surprisingly touching and enrich the narrative. A fine achievement.

Prof. Duane Locke: (Professor Emeritus & Poet in Residence; University of Tampa)

There is much to praise in Corkish's extraordinary autobiographical poem but I will single out his inventive prosody; it is the prosody of typographical music. Especially notable is his letter shading, from subtle colours to pale greys that co-exist with varied fonts, white spaces, and an abundance of other devices. The pages not only excite with their visual impact, but his visual materiality becomes communicative, functions as a chorus to expand meaning beyond the literality of the words producing a poetically meaningful referential song.

Lorette C. Luzajic: (Canadian artist and poet, creator of *The Idea Factory*)

If it happened, it happened to Alan Corkish. Beginning with his entrance into the world in a small fishing town at the same time as Hiroshima was being torn apart by an atomic bomb, the poet's autobiographical recordings observe world historical events from one man's view. And this man observes everything; witches, aliens, political corruption, philosophy, serial killers, nothing escapes Corkish's intense scrutiny. In this unfinished symphony of a life, with recollections firmly planted in the backdrop of history, Corkish re-educates us in the events we have forgotten by weaving the news bulletins into the poetry of human emotions and conflicts. At turns violent, sad, erotic, triumphant, funny... *Glimpses of Notes* recalls history as if it had a soul.

Dr. Anil K Prasad: (Indian poet; Head of English at Ibb University; Yemen)

Alan Corkish's *Glimpse of Notes* is a brilliant synthesis of imagination, reason and orthographic exploitation which amalgamates into a unique lyricism. His rhythm and idiom is put into appropriate and sometimes shocking structural variations which accentuate the poetic potentialities of the English language. Corkish knows his craft well and never indulges in sentimentality. His poetic paintings of epic span and depth are enthralling. *Glimpses* is everyman's 'record of which I am.' The semantic universe of the poem lies not only in the lines but also between the lines - ironically compressed, carefully carved, painted, and performed through words which dance and make the reader dream of a past when 'steel fibres/ screaming of/gulls and winches/glimpses of notes/' echo through the corridors of time. Superb creativity, a rhythmic creation of beauty through the use of technology which makes the words 'speak' to the reader. The poem urges the reader to go on and on reading, reflecting and re-evaluating the words which reverberate like the ripples created in the quiet space of unconsciousness.

Sam Smith: (Novelist and poet; editor of *The Journal*)

Given the cast of characters, vernacular accurately rendered, those who formed Corkish's character are lyrically not that far removed from those in *Under Milkwood*. A *Milkwood* here, however, with no romantic/macho illusions about the intake of alcohol; nor the perpetuation of respectable/acceptable politics. Quaint *Glimpses* aint. Consequences are explored and lived with, endured. These pages bite. He says that 'a book that isn't worth burning is not worth reading'. Go pore over *Glimpses of Notes* by candlelight in a puddle of petrol.

Prof. Robert Sheppard: (UK poet-critic; Professor at Edge Hill University)

There are two systems of meaning at play in *Glimpses of Notes*. There is the voice that button-holes us, telling us a life-story, like the *Ancient Mariner*, offering its opinions and pointing towards footnotes to historicize itself. It is a voice that is an irritant to our complacency. The other meaning is for our eyes. Beneath what we read there is a wild meaning, dwelling in the shapes, spacing and splicing of words and, of course, in their colours. Sometimes it counterpoints the life-story told here; sometimes it resists it with a precision of its own, a life of its own. I invite you to read this double-life.

L. Ward Abel: (Georgian poet and musician)

The voice of Alan Corkish in this epic tempts us towards a threshold of self-discovery through which we accompany this brilliant conjurer of honesty and whimsy onward to his new world of strange words. His structural approach to poetry is unique but has the power of Joyce's introspection. Through the anti-climax of Post War Britain, and despite poverty, illness and demons, Corkish emerges as a hero in this autobiography: stronger for the battle, a weary but eloquent dreamer. This is a truly important work.

Not to Explain, but to Assist

What follows is arguably part of a conversation following on from the pause you made just prior to turning the page or choosing to open this book. You have the power to interrupt whenever you so desire in the same way that you have the option to exercise this same power at any stage of your journey throughout this whole document. As stated; this is not an explanation of the poem, it is intended to assist only.

Contemplate the written word; especially the transcript and amalgamation of text and paper which chooses to label itself as poetry. It is, in most instances, a mere fragment of what poetry should be. Endeavouring to uncover a fresh format I began to look at the visual properties of regular text and increasingly began to find the formats unsatisfactory, due mainly to their predictability and conformity. Words and phrases constitute poetry but there is little aesthetically pleasing in a word or phrase per se. Surely the function of the poet is to create more than words and more than random concrete pictures with words. Ponder this complex question which I asked myself prior to writing 'Glimpses of Notes'; is it possible to blend structure, fonts and the fragmented trace-roots of words into something that lends differing infrastructure to the words as visualised, creating new superstructures that will allow a poem or a series of words, phrases and the paper they are part of, to be viewed from different angles, in different lights, in differing columns of words-within-words separated by purposeful font-changes or rhythmically fragmented shades of black and white, or even colour? With this question foremost I began to write.

When I began writing I was also reading everything that came to hand. However the cynicism of poets like Larkin and Eliot, and their palpable contempt for ordinary people, alienated me initially from the undoubted poetic quality of their work and so I began to look more closely at the actual structure of poetic works. I was bemused at just how 'ordinary' most poetic styles were, constantly plodding onwards using the same techniques that had gone before. Eliot annoyed by constantly picking up on religious references and with his inability to conceal his contempt for the hollow men, and Larkin too was busy being Larkin, sneering perpetually at his Mr. Bleaney, lecturing us eternally about restraint; creating private electric fences. But although I grew to appreciate Eliot as an artist my annoyance continued and was not confined to the mere content of poetry.

I read also the alleged 'new poets'. At their best, they use language and the framing of text wittily and intellectually, although it surprises me how often the form is incestuously reductionist and so very commonplace. It was soon clear that most of these alleged new poets lacked humanity, warmth and, above all, a political voice although notable exceptions occur; Robert Sheppard and Allen Fisher spring to mind. It has also to be said that when some modern poets resort to the 'concrete' the shape of text in some instances seems arbitrary and is perhaps used without giving a great deal of thought to the completed composition except on the basic-level of creating text as a cross (in a poem about a crucifixion) or a penis (in a poem about sex). I use that word again and make no excuses for that; most of it is 'ordinary' and predictable, almost as though on one hand they cannot see what has gone before and so subconsciously and by almost subliminal default they unconsciously emulate and plagiarise the giants; or they stand on the shoulders of great poets gazing back over the panoply seeking permission to continue but seldom actually moving forward.

Another unfortunate trend with the 'New Poets', is the downward slide into obscure textual references and/or an over-intellectualising of the text to the extent that even well-educated people are frequently alienated. These are people who apparently are happy only when they are reveling in their superior knowledge of language and their academic prowess, people who call a spade a 'levering and redistributing insertion mechanism.' The resultant alleged poetry is read and distributed amongst perhaps a dozen or less 'intellectuals' and their dog who meet monthly in Ye Olde Glue Pot to discuss 'progress' without realising that there has not been any. Invariably what is produced is obscure **un**poetry understood only as part of a private, tribal, pseudo-academic, language.

To me poetry is an intensely personal and visual thing and therefore I have little empathy with modern 'performance' poets (a young student at a poetry reading recently revealed wisdom beyond her years when she went to the microphone and said; 'If you stand up here and say any old rubbish loudly and confidently people will applaud…' and the assembled audience, entirely unconscious of the irony, duly applauded her). I accept that poems should occasionally be read aloud, some indeed are designed to be read aloud; these are mainly light and/or humourous anecdotes, not what I would deem to call 'poetry'. In the main most modern poetry readings are pleasurable in the same way that masturbation is pleasurable; fleeting, more a relief than a culmination of a loving experience, somehow ultimately deeply **un**satisfying. What is often forgotten is that the English language is filled with wonderful nuances that can only be appreciated through viewing the words on paper. One example of this is the Donald McGill post card which portrays a shocked gentleman overhearing two substantial ladies enlarging on the merits of their respective babies; one says; 'He's like his father, lungs like bellows and <u>bawls</u> like a bull!' Speak that out loud and it means nothing, view it and it has meaning.

My own poetry in places bawls like a bull for I also have something to say over-and-above the way my poetry appears. I hope it is never simply 'pretty' although I do have egotistical dreams of my poetry erupting concrete from the earth forming the bulwarks of solid pillars with voices or music intruding at some lesser level. Poetry literally cut in stone or inlaid into translucent pillars curved like giant half bananas which rise from the floor to tower some two or three feet above the reader. A viewer/reader stops at a pillar and as s/he closes in to focus on the text faint voices intrude... (but that is in dreams, and my school reports did say that I have an overactive imagination). What is actually being affirmed in 'Glimpses of Notes' is on one hand a personal and private comment on the way my own life has been effected-by or has interspersed-with history and on the other hand is a comment on that same history framed within the place I occupy therein. Thus it is also a political statement, a social statement and a reflection as to what all of 'this' means to all of 'you'; the human-beings who occupied and shared that same past space.

The autobiographical poem I present herein is experimental and, in a sense, incomplete; the reader views it as it is to date, ostensibly an unfinished work. Indeed it is a tautology that no autobiographical work can never be finished. On the whole I am relatively happy with the structure and the content but have something to confess with regard to the notion of integrity, which should be foremost in an autobiography; there are things I shun away from because there are times when my life, my 'self' if you will, was unacceptable both to me and to others. The problem, with regard to the sticky question of honesty in autobiography, is that I may well write a line which may be interpreted as '...at this point in time I stopped beating my wife...' but, as Eliot might have it; 'That is not it at all, That is not what I meant, at all.' However if I have strayed from honesty in the content of what follows it is merely by way of omission or the kind of false recollection referred to in 'Part 11' and never through intentionally falsely presenting facts.

At one level, by tradition, poetry should explore, analyse and intellectualise but at its most primitive or basic level it merely exposes the nerves of raw emotion within. In 'Glimpses of

Notes' I've set about the task of producing an entire image, the image of, what I know to have been, an eventful life. Errors of interpretation will undoubtedly occur but that is because the reader is part of the process, has occupied the same space and the same history. The poem **is** *autobiographical* but it is not necessarily *factual* thus any reader's interpretation may well be more correct than my own recollections.

The art form I have attempted to produce should ideally come across as textual, pictorial, aural, visual, pleasing to the ear, the eye and the intellect but above all as a representation of honest emotions. Each nuance of text, shading and colour has a purpose which is not entirely or merely an alienation technique, although I do use an accusatory questioning to constantly remind the reader that it is at least an interpretation of reality I am dealing with. (As in the recurring refrain; 'You; could you sing?') Nor is it Schlovsky either but a new 'way of seeing' via defamiliarised layout which, incidentally, makes close reading essential. Perhaps it challenges Schlovsky's notion that art should make the stone stony in that what I try to do is make the stone stonier. A sacrilegious thought intrudes here; perhaps if we can't do better than God, there is no point to art…?

Finally; complexity of text or language is not desirable in itself although we must commit ourselves to using the tools we have at our disposal, ('words' and a 'page' in which to inlay these 'words'), to their most aesthetically and intellectually pleasing extent. I hope that 'Glimpses of Notes' steers clear of complex, pseudo-intellectual phraseology and is accessible, at least at some level, to anyone who chooses to view it.

With the above in mind I offer 'Glimpses of Notes', a work in progress. It is a simple and uncomplicated story with a beginning and a middle and, at some time, an end. I suspect though that, if at some distant date I eventually declare it to be 'finished' you will still not have a fully clothed picture... but I hope that is not the case. 'Glimpses' is a skeleton that I have attempted to flesh out, I am however aware of its limitations.

Finally may I ask you, the reader, to bear in mind a Chinese proverb; '...the longest journey begins with a single step...' bear with me... and, as I say towards the end of this fragment of a poem; 'Watch this space', if fate allows, there is more to come.

Alan Corkish; September 2013

Part '1' PRELUDE

...the **vanity** of life demands
a record of all that i am
and so a
beginning;

on a day of quiet gladness;
Mannin is calm, and veiled
in misty rain.

we approach
Ramsey bay seaward
enter between the twin stone piers
to catch a protective harbour
bullwarked by the
mist-drizzled

pine-splattered **Lhergy Frizzle**
Sky Hill and North **Bar**rule...

on the deck of the SS Conister
}docked near the Customs House{
sarwester-clad
'Fly' Cotcha
[teeth biting at the stem
of his clay-pipe]
whistles up
the steam winches
as Jack the Knife
and Brother Fisher haul-to
on the guys
another net from
the hold beneath;

gin, farm fodder, factory bearings,
tractor-parts,
overalls, paint... all smelling
of fire... smoke... war...
~~~~this; The Living Boat
a weekly tripper~~~~

and close to, near The Commie,
the Ben Maye rolls, Billy the
Gull organises **the Big Six**
to muscle from its depths
400 tons of coals from the

Manchester Ship Canal

fishing boats lie three abreast; the
Cushag, the Snaefell, the
Zulu Warrior,
~~~~

holds alive with cod,
hake, john-dory, monkfish
ripple and bob as the Master Frank
steams outward laden with lobster pots.

By Cowley's the Ben Ain
lolls
with *steaming* paper bags of
cement from Larne
and the quay-s
i
d
e
even at this early h*our*
alive with children, Danish
fishermen, unloading~gangs,
intermerrying-women
with gutting ~ knives
sheltering in pub door
ways,
sorters; piling high the
cockle-sacks near the
chain railings,
the rattle of
steel fibres
and the **screaming**
of **gulls** and ***winches***
glimpses of notes echo
as cordite... and powder-smoke
mingle in the salt-swept air

today

in this **my town-to-be**
-born-in

on a November morning

Part '2' INNOCENCE

Mother
struggled with
our birth while
Christie 1
was killing
in Rilling
ton
Place...

first memories
slippery as slugs
tiptoeing like vague
silhouettes of shadows
a tortoiseshell cat as big as me
under the woollen table cloth's
shade
lino... cold and worn
and coloured blocks
on a tin truck
the box above the
open hearth that sang
and somehow
a depth of sadness
came from it too and
everyone sat silent as the word
Hiroshima seeped into my 2
undeveloped brain

riotous Saturdays;
pubs closed an' **singin'**
-in-the-lane
on Jack Crick's shoulders
as he wades through
knee - deep
moon - stained
snow
then... everyone stops talkin'
about aliens 3
and begin dancin':-
feet **flyin'**
hokey
cokeying into number-4
past the V of that
woollen table-
cloth {with me beneath... laffin...
*...and yer left leg's in Auntie
Scag... an' i can see yer
pale **pink** knickers...*}

crates piled high by
the pantry door and
either side
of the **h**earth close by...
reaching out to purloin
a **Mackeson** (cos
it's **'good for u'**)
and laughing at
'Brother Sylves**t**'
[#~who has a punch
that could sink a battleship~
big ship!~#] 4
which booms ***bass*** as tin-legged
war-hero
Uncle
Archie
swings mum high by
the gas mantle's
gentle
hissssssss sssss sss s ssssssssss

slate **grey** slabs
and cobbles mingle
either side of a gutter where
RugMat the whip**pet**
drinks and the sun
struggles to creep
down into the **narrowness**
touches briefly
a **brass** tap...
the curled wrought
iron mangle with
its **yellowed**
and splintered
wood
rollers
at the walls
dead ||
end ||
and where
a boy of five ~~~ bare-foot

[red-hair
short
back-and-sides
ruffled]
sits on a
s*a*n*d -stone step

inhaling the scent
of poverty
reading the cartoon
strips in the Daily Sketch
sport's page reveals Russian Hero
wins The National 5

(and Mum had 6d E.W.on it
tinned salmon for tea...)

Shelley [mother of
a thousand kittens]
lies close by
squints skywards
purrs like the coal-black
kettle on the leaded grate and
rolls her rows
of soft pink nipples to the warmth
of his ab~sent
out~stretched hand

[~...and, on the flicks, at
The Plaza,

a fat-man on a ferris
wheel
is talkin' about
Cuckoo Clocks...~] 6

an early memory from the child's eyes sees
Mrs Nicky, twentieth century witch,
hurtling down *Water* Street
~hair and cape f l y i n g~
on a cast-iron bike
harmonising with the cobbles
mangling unwary cats
causing Blind Neddy's
horse to rear...

elbows jutting and black dots of eyes
fixed fast ahead with that chin
and nose almost meeting like
rusting caliper arms...
off to read a teacup
or organise a spuggie 7
to terrify the neighbours ~

{Fear death by water... 8
everyone...
those be pearls that
are Abbey's eyes...} 9

~ and in a clamourous second
she's gone, [and didn't catch
me looking]
with purple
potent
and {*dark*}ly-scented
herbs falling from the
rear saddle basket leaving a
snail-like trail to delineate
all that she ruled
over

Religion

...the opium of... 10

intruded
rare\ly
confined to collecting
ship half-pennies for the Sally
who sold fish;
three halfpence
a dish
or trem*bli*ng with
The Shakers in College
Street
or stealing fruit and veg
from the baskets
laid out at
the Altar in
ro
the Seaman's B/e\thel
at Harvest Festival
time

but reading **genesis** furtively
after Sunday school
i dis*cover*ed
that Onan
fucked his
brother's wife, 11
then
had an attack of conscience

and came his **dust**
into
the
dust,
~~~which was a **good**
thing to have done~~~
& the **Omniscient Lord**
whom we worshipped on Sundays
witnessed all
and was concerned for ‘the wa**st**ed seed’
so he slew Onan

not for his lust
~understand~
but for his attack of conscience

discovered therefor;

...the heart
of a heartless world... 12

God is
an
Amoral Bastard
realised;
God would
not fit the battle against the
Black Pig
who even then was
settling his sharp hooves
whispering his
sweetly un-understandable
and
obscene
blasphemies;

‘ten out of ten
births
result in
death’

‘Don’t go over The Tip’ said ***Weegy-Wise-One***
‘oh yeh’
‘the place is crawling with *chinks*
haven’t you heard it on the wireless? The
little yellow Koreans are over there killing 13
each other... it’s right (*cos it feels good*); they 14
~~~

came in boots to Jurby Beach stay away and
leave those rats
alone...'

so we did;
for a day or two,
then it was back to
breathlessly night-hunting
the Long Tailed Fellas
with torches
and catapults
unny now we called them
'Chinky-Reds'

on Maughold rocks
gathering gulls' eggs
for Skillicorn's bakery
with the Manx shearwaters &
the slit-throat razor-bills
the preening puffin mods
birds with familiar names and colours that filled
my childhood/~
~\senses like psychedelic overtures or
preludes ~~ glimpses
and the great green blue
froth-corrupted sea below ~~~~~~~ waiting patiently
for
someone

sandwiched
between two half-sisters ~
half sawn bean *tins*

}like uncle Archie's
under the bed *legs*
*fill*ed with paraffin 15
fill my senses
beside me - in the night -
a mouse on the
bare boards scuttling
and chomping the darkness
in the attic above me
~always~
goosie ankle-stomps her 16
melancholy//\\torment
[out~side
in the cobbled lane
a beautiful Tennessee Waltz 17
sidles to me through
a cracked window; Joe Cherry's
voice calls
'Marciano done **Louis**...'] 18
A N D
in the moon-scoured night
above the salt-line
hare bells struggle
{ruffian nature at **Gale** Force eight
bullies and molests their
slender stems}
...and far, far away
Zero is being asked
is he now
or has he ever been... 19
as i lie wide-eyed and sleepless
watching for the

dawn

there is a gnome in
old **Shoof**ler's garden
and **Shoof**ler's missus
zes it's him... watching...

El Sid, the
morgue man

told us it was trUe coz
his death-ashes had
been mixed with
Portland cement
an' stuffed into the
mould;

we looked back then
with greater respect at
old **Shoof**ler with his
green fishing rod
and **bright** red
pointed hat...
watching-smiling
more powerful now in death
than he ever was in shuffling life...

an' none of us scrumped
in **his** garden...

what

...but Aunt Cissie and my mother
sat and cried 20
when they heard on the wire\less

that Uncle Jo' died

the tables were set up 21
in the lane
between the washing
and some t **a** t **t** e **r** e **d**
bunting ~~~ we
scoffed soda bread and
marge with jam on too
and at school
i got a mug with *her*
face on it *for free* which
Frank and uncle
Jack topped up
throughout the
sun-drenched day with warm
mild beer from a huge brown jug
the mug lasted
about a week until
the handle came of *f*
in the wash and then
mum placed it in the
window-sill with some
dandelions in it
...a few months after that
it became a target for
Cliffy's catapult

matinee Saturdays
and five hundred
kids [where do
they all come from]
crowing and
cackling at the
Pathe News
cockerel

but didn't
Flash Gordon actually
fall right into ***The Pit of***
Fire
last week
Johnny MacBrown
?

Uncle Benny
London-gangster
flash-ties
pencil 'tash
and a wicked **black .38**
showed me
breathe-stopping beauty
in a half-inch
long deep **scarlet**
and **black**
fetal curled bean...
hollowed and
minutely hinged
inside;
carved from
a chip of ivory,
a perfect
African elephant
that still comes to me
pale~ly
cream~ly
like the catch
of a song
in dreams

visions of boyhood
expand;
around midnights... with
Jack Jackson
and his cat... or
Luxxy
(dial at Hilversum)
crackling a **pop**
top
twenty
thick white poker
toast
smoking by
the stove-coal fire

dipped in
sweet connie-onnie
laced
tea like glue
in Tom's~~~

green-cardiganed Kathy,
un~speaking,
on the set==tee

'something' happened to her

Stone PIER; Ramsey
summer sun
beating down on
nakedness
tasting air-salt
{**stolen Golding
newly thumbed and
wrapped
safe
in my patched towel by the
BullRocks**}
and the two foot
wide concrete wall
with Yucky pedalling
[me on the handlebars]
then launched off

into the bre
ath snatchin'

Gut tumbling

s p a c e

~~~~~~

before
the green water rushed
up and closed over my screams
i saw a one-eyed fat boy
and a pig's head on a stick
mocking
and a woman on the end of
a rope with her
tongue
lolling 22
then sinking down
wondering
if this time
[That's the way with the kids , you know,] 23
they'd let me
drown
{like brother Abbey who...
...on a still March evening
following a mackerel sky...
couldn't s~w~i~m
either}

but scrumping and trapping
not fun
not always echoes of dreamland
\not always Press button 'B'
and
get yer money back/
~:~
necessity.
N*ecessity*
filling an empty **belly**
stopped wedding **cars (begging)**
[by any other name]
rabbits foot gnawed free
left in a brass loob and
trailed blood
no food this week 'Frank didn't work...'
turnips thieved and gnawed
[sweet *yellow***ness]**
rewarded with lashed bare legs from a Switch
and gut-ache
duck's h^d ead torn from
~~~~~~

feathered warmth by loob
coal, sticks and fish trawled
in a barrow door-to-door
'2d a bundle for kindlin' lady,
nice fresh fish 2 bob...'
fed on (force fed) Cruelty
/~...when the clock strikes two...~\
Thieving,
/~...three...~
Begging
/~...and four...~\
made-to
and punished thus
to grow *warped* or to accept
Injustice
?
{it's a strange journey into this brief space Snowy} 24
Now... Lady Mad-donna-smith, {Janie's eldest}
[as one JD 25
bows out]
see how it r u n s :

Part '3' GROWING UP

Suez surprised us [26]
rattling
over the
radio waves
John's roaring
Bull
castrated
~ though Uncle Jack said
we should
kick the wog's arse;
give him some *cold*-steel ~----
.....later
i learnt that garrotter Gamel
has his hands on **The**
Empire's throat
a singular punishment for yet
another broken promise
no real tears shed here though
as
the imperialist
death throes danced on
black and white television
screens and
the kids on the streets were
ashamed of what they saw
the last limp gesture
from a senile lion's paw
even then
i felt the guilt
c r e e p i n g ~ felt even then
we were **wrong**

what sort of a man 27
was this that strutted onto

the stage of life to keep the adults ~

all hands over mouths ~ talking and giggling

'the summit of sex -

the pinnacle of masculine, feminine,

and neuter... a

deadly, winking,

sniggering, snuggling,

chromium-plated,

scent-impregnated,

luminous, quivering, giggling,

fruit-flavored, mincing,

ice-covered heap of mother love...'

In the dock he denied his

sexuality...

a cowardly act?

more or less

cowardly then

than the

cold + unfeeling

society which

forced him to lie?

and anyway; Mum loved him

and laughed when he

cried all the way to the bank

Smithy and i
were scientists. In his
back bedroom we
manipulated toilet roll
innards and chrome tubes
with the heap of old spectac**le**
lenses we'd found on the tip
high motives of course
for with the constructed
[though blurred]
four foot telescope
we could watch
Elsa and **the**
Anderson girls getting
ch**a**nged by the gorse patch on the Sulby river
and charge
Gedda and Pawnee
a penny each to
lOOk

[but we couldn't see the tanks
rolling in to Hungary] 28

what is

for ***Kathy***, who never spoke,
the r~i~v~e~r stood still
and land ~~~~~~~~~ flowed
by on either side
she

endured li*f*e

spoke
only **after** d e a t h
only to

ME

Diana and Vicky
14 so
'older women'
in the
sweet-scented
long-grass
-field at midni ght
fumblings
both beneath me
c o o l **l o n g**
fingers exploring
(#...Oh please
stay by me... Diana...#) 29
so intensely that
the explosion
blasts me to
my feet then
run
n
ing
run
n____ing
ru nnnnnn in g...
...and in the bath
room checking i was
OK
and then doing
it daily/severally
...they both changed then
too and midnight **sign**als
brought them
singularly to the
cat plagued alley to pant
and deny
and suc-cum

(also)watchingallthe
[girlsgoby]
factorygirlsflowingshortskirtsrevealing
milkwhitethighswrappedinstockings
leftarmrestingonwoodenwindowsill
fixedfacesmiletryingnottoeyepop
righthandwritesbehindthebrickwork
knowingsomethingshouldhappen
[butnotwhat]
andtheupturnedfacessmilingandwaving
andguessing[idiscoveredlater]mysolitarypursuit

Summer night-silent
still
hea t pounding **i**
levered at ste|a|el windows
and
inside the .303 rifles' 'n
bayonets
were prime.

/Some 'silver' cups aS
trophies ------------but wE
couldn't find the subs-boX|

in court Tom and i
puzzled over the £6. 8. and threepence
'costs'
'til it dawned that Nighting**ale** Teddy
had gone back for another look
and we were **expec**ted to pay
£2. 2 and 9 comp...

bastard *Ted* got it
though going down for
three while i
[being the baby]
sidled free
'cept for the wrath
of mother and big Jim...
...and of course...

the name notched
yet again

in the opposition'sssSS
boooo...ks

turnip-dock-ing dock-scythe swings 30
/hammered revulsion\
bruised moot
tops **purpled**

coloured vein
as Sputnik bleeps over 31

Frost entered digit tips
sliced
Juice **Blood**
m i n g l e
back achingly rhythmic ~

creaking **rooks** harsh mockly ~
sack-wrapped bitterly\
\shutten-bleak-winds
all rheumy bluster
thins vision
to underwater blur
^bunking school
for this?^
{but Kerouac beats on 32
his road too though
we're paid by the yard so
not one of
the most Magic/**est** PC
Moments eh? } 33
***youcouldyou*sing**

my small town floats
in its own
reality and **outside**{r} **in the night**
strange creatures walk through
their private dreams **outside of the**
frame

Mopochatcha Pocket Snatcher
in pork-pie hat; greatcoat
ending one inch
above his polished boots stands
erect in
Pegram's door way
smoking a woodbine
lit by a gas-street-lamp
Malcolm the allsort-
addict passes **carrying his bike out**
cos it carried him in
Scrange the Whistler
emerges
tall and slim as a birch rod
floating upwards through the *slats*
in the grid
whistling onwards fingers jam*med*
beneath his tongue
sending his ***private melodies***
into the ***night scented air***
as
Scoops in

woo\den clogs
bends to hear
what junior ***Shoofler*** with his

inherited
d e f o r m ed feet is whispering
and finds he is singing softly
along with ***Scrange***
a cat scrambles over ***Irvine's*** wall
looking for fishheads
and a lone **dog pads**
up the narrowlane from
the coal-flecked quayside
home to naked ***Mrs Trotter***
and ***Geddawook*** for war**m**
milk and r a b b i t meat
to curl up after on the patchworked
bed
with the heat of the iron-oven-door
in a tea cloth beneath

'existence is use-
-less Descarte'

...in her lone bed
across the landing
mother murmurs to my absent
father
&
on South beach
a curlew calls
to three new stars
for that would be
the day {~ay~ay}
that
Ritchie, BB
'n sweet Buddy I
Idied [34]

salmon-poaching; [35]
soft but
foldly rippling
and the river-skeined **weed**
protecting
and the tail end South
moving timidly
knees damp
back arched over the
reflectiveness
wild gar**lic** in the lungs
hand-**shaded** eye
tight-screwed
seek s prized
alien
raining in d**rople**ts
disturbed by the
moor-hen's

pa**dd**le-web foot
and stabbing yellow*ness*
stillness
brings
no relief to the elbowed long dip
cold
digits intruding

it is~~~~~~~~~~ʇı sı

reflecting
again
tickling but
not laughter here
(in ark-ed disarray
skyward sails)
flounders
knowing the first **h e a t**
knife~ripping
belly **hotly**

y**o**uc**o**uldyousing

Kipper, Bing, Shakey
and the rest in the
Pool Ballroom
swirling Saturday
nights with Little
Richard
belting *Long Tall Sally*
and swirling skirts flashing
knickers
and suspenders

B**e**e-hive hair do's
bobbing
and me with my D.A.
combing through the brylcream
carefully in the
bog
slicking the sideboards back...
un-safety raZors stitched
beneath the collars of my
three quarter length
powder blue coat

a **mini-deemster**
specking me thrOugh
short-
-sighted
lenses
~one of those little ***things***
sent to try us~
spluttered at me
in Peel Caught
\room/
while mum sobbed
and Spud sat head-in-
disbelieving hands
~~giving me
my character in no uncertain
form and
then handing out his
Justice:
You will be
fined money
bound over
cur**few**ed
jai**led**
bir**ch**ed... 36
} the quality of mercy
was not strained ~~~ it was 37
broad sieved {
should i have told him that the
machine which has brought us to
our present rung in
the evolutionary ladder
stems from violence?
perhaps not... ~ but i did
...and the little grub
did**n't** say
'you will be
labeled...
for ever...'
{do i frighten you that much?}
but i en**visa**ged him
unw**rapp**ing
Dealer's shit~
~bomb
and i smiled

[so he banned me
from the City
for a YEAR!]
HEADLINE

38

rabbit-ing
firmly barruled
beneath wind-ripped
reflecting light n battery
heavily strapped n dogs silent
n **bloody** draped carcases heavy
lung scorching

heat
from
body
ripped
\
\
\
as **downthe**down n down
n thud of heavy boots
with light dancing then
stopped straight
to beam **eye** direction
n snap
as quickly
n
move
on
as
quickly
and the wind~~~rolling
and the breath like
stick~~~~~le~backs

Hairpin = van waiting
n
two hundred guts
tumble ‘n
all at 9d a lb plus pelts

youcouldyousing

Peter the Painter

Ticket of Leave
Terrorist
[absconded

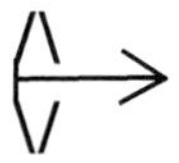

snuck in via
Jurby Beach]
taught me and Kenny
to sing
Kevin Barry
in Gerry's candle-lit flat
above the brook
with the dozens of car-battery-
operated tv's piled high
silently tuned
Into
everything
When all was
Black and White
[naive perfection]
&
we drank
Bushmills
with hot-sugared water from
the kettle on the open fire
played chess
til late
and put the
World to Rights

in our cell above Douglas
Busi-Station
{**Peter Mac** & **Bulla**
carved in the table
+
pigeons cooing
beneath the barred windows}
sporting our **b*i*rch**-marks
just back from ironing the
billiard tables in the Police-Club
and feeding the dogs by the Quay

Quivers and i took a
fight which was so intense that
the bed collapsed...

Higgins rushed in
cane in *h*and
plodding
minions in tow
and the look he gave us
....suggested....
in any case; by
that evening we had
separate cells

'something untoward...

is going on...' **we heard**
Old Higgins say ~

but in reality
it was only kindly Frank and Jim
with their pink Manchester
caddie and their
lame lamb Larry
who ever fancied
Quivers or me

that-way

corn-drying 39
split two
24 hours
bagging hot ness
and then sling-hacking
200lb **sack**loads
up up up [the
steel beams ***rusted*** ness]
whirry fan
-driven
furnaced air poll~di~luted
pollen gassed
chokeladen night
foggly seen through
septemberish dark and **light**
then **re**
\\doled

you ***couldyousing***
[am asking]
what is it

first job after being expelled 40
& leaving King's Lynn beet factory
we'd drawn all our back pay;
insisted on pound and ten-bob
notes - eleven weeks graft on
twelve hour shifts netted over
£600.00 and now all there was to
do was blow it...
pulling into
Newcastle Central we saw
him alone on the midnight plat
form ~ the slow falling snow had
formed a heavy crust on his
stooped shoulders and beneath
his great coat he'd tied news
papers with hairy string... the
V beneath his heavy beard
revealed a Daily Mail head
line announcing Macmillan's 41
s l o g a n

"That poor bugger's never had it
so good" **Big G remarked -**

it took ten seconds to split our

wad and i leapt back on the train
as it crawled to speed and we
pressed our faces to the cold
glass watching but he didn't move
just sat still as though frozen part
of the concrete landscape amidst the
fading streaks of
mid
December
snow
f
a
ll
\
\
\
\ 42

cement-backing
the paper heat
greyly blistering
leaking silli chotic dUst

traffic !**no entry**!
work at manliness
running -both laden and-
un
[sacks]
paper
steps
to
silk-ruddled rafters\
achingly high
and at **night** then
iced **anaesthetic**
skinscreaming **blood**pounding

suffering for one day

like Mandela would for thirty years

youcouldyousing

Magic Abebe
head floating 43
above a body
that moved with an
irresistible
rhythm
not too long a stride
eating distance in a
way that betrayed

no hint of e x e r t i o n
flowing momentum neither   coldly efficient
nor   aggressive
nor   ruthless
never   tiring
running   his own race
eyes fixed on
the finish
from the
first pace
no one passed   him
no one had the   legs
the   heart
the   eyes

17   and shut off from rea**lit**y
heavy with dark rum i guided her
to the house on
the hill where the
grotesquely named   Dr Hook 
waited with his
torn sheets ~ cotton-
wool ~
hot-water   and   that
fisherman's knife   with the
brass clasp that made her   recoil
into my arms
gagging with the   fumes
from the pad ~~~
standing above her
holding tight to one hand   stifling
her screams with that
vomit-inducing ether
for close to two hours
until
his eyes   dark and fear-filled
told me it was over...

afterwards i filled the carrier bags
with blooded scraps as she
laced a cotton pad between her
legs; shoulders-rocking... retching...
sobbing...
hand-on-bruised-distended-stomach...
and then i picked up
a globule and wiped it clean

perfectly curled in that
foetal position
three inches long
with sightless orbs for eyes
and perfect toes and fingers...

NOW; forty years on
i see it still; its eyes now
are blue and can see
the real me, the one who
planned and executed
no point in refusing
to accept
in arguing that i am
not **he**, feebly urging that **he**
has gone totally
...every atom and molecule...
for i know that something
intangible is still the same and
so i accept the accusing stare
a reminder of the continuity
of my life
and the finality of its

do not enter 44

the quarantine

zone *says*

McNamara

i was one month

short of eighteen

convinced

beyond doubt

that that day was

my last on earth

Billy Stole and me
in The Commy
dressed in drainies
pink drape-jackets
blue brothel-creepers
and bootlace ties
drunk an' singing
If yerv gotta to make
a fool o' somebo,ooody.... 45
urging Flo 'n Fred to tell the
'phone
callers
***we're not here*; Jean**
and Esme cuddling
giggling
but as the Ben Maye
steamed in to harbour at
mid*night*
the *Pea*-Picker
frothed
and Swaley from the Office said;
Get back on board yusser **or**
yer sacked
~~~drunk we told him
ter stick his rust-shite ship
but when she sailed
for cement in Larne
next ~~tide~~

Bill was c a s t i n g off
and i was sweating ale
in the stoko...

[...THEN ~ on the radio;
***Bang, Bang, Bang*,**
and Catholic Jack's dead.... 46

{the Chief said it was Lee
'hiding in a
sup~posi~tory!'}]

and....
~~~ **stoking meant: slaked on carb**
ripping arc
through bleeding heat ~
naked~ [47]
ashFined
re-rasping
harsh spilt sputum
sweatly **cooled~tea**
and root hairs
frizzlingly torture
popping flesh like **prickly**
need les(**s**)
deep against heaving metal
full jacketed protection
from **ocean**-mid-
waves raked salt-choking
and lungly-ripped **hot**ness
youcould***yousing***

every single night when
the Pubs closed it
was **poker**
at someone's pad
[often m**i**ne]
with Gerry,
fingering his cravat,
'Snot' dealing / card draw
Pete rigging the deck
and Fat-Andy smiling
[...unless ***mad***-Lucy
dealt 'shoot'...]
...and the sweat
and the table stakes
un *believ*able now
looking back
real **Blue Chips** [48]
and always folding on
the *dead*-man's hand [49]
but sweating and adrenalin
was the hook
like the night
~~~

at Pete Mac's winning close
to 4,000 quid (£££)
and then {**brim**ming
with it} agreeing
to cut double or
quits x2 or 0

with that f**a**t farmer
from The Lhen

the three of clubs
i turned
~~~ so i walked
out
Pete told me later
at work (£3.15.6 a week)
the bastard drew ***a one***
eyed jack...
{but i was back there
for
The Sweat} that same night

&
Irene and i...
we lay softly together
the summer - moon's cool breath,
a gazelle's eyes

Kibbutz Niram when
Vodka and Ice meant
six whole oranges juiced
as a side order and
when **Dee** and Tom bust
up and i took her swim
ming
in the hot salted
ness
and,
with her thighs on
my shoulders,
in the cool orange grove i
tasted the
hot salt-sweet
ness
of her

...she was my world and every
breath i take...
~~~

sun-beat broke backs
towards noon but i
worked on spreading
the brown sticky mortar on the
white heat of those
ungraceful stones which would
never sit straight... and paid...
skin stripped
and that
feeling of helpless nausea
that told you n/ever...
[again]
laughter of children in our
bunkrooms at **sunset**
with Jericho **teaching**
them to **sing**
or to **play**
his **mandolin**
chords
which would
enter
in their own
time **tripping**
the fading **corridors**
of **memory**
voices
never to be heard
echoes of dreamland
again tumbling over the
speakers insistent
call to prayer
flitting through
a sullied mind thirty
years hence

coal-digging:
ceiling-iron first in hold
(scrape shuffled pairs follow
and me teamed with Brother Fisher:
'this'll gerra back on yer' as he sucks
on a pint of cold-tea)
muscles cryin *Gulls* screamin
(but fade as diurnal deafness
plagues an tin en**tombs**)
backnots **black**ly straighten
twelve hours *in*

and vaseline **sta*in*ed**
below eye stra*in***ed**
burnsssssssssssssssss

in ton iron ~ steam-winched
tubs
carrying from
darkled **dust**-shot **sh*ade*** to **sun** -
f*ade*
6d a ton

you***couldyou***sing

who

...laced with **L**
S
D
i took Anne's
child
upon my k**nee**
~Monk's Brilliance
hovering in the Corners
of my senses~
and shook the
Qualtrough's lemonade
bottle until the bubbles
gushed **explosively**
and i giggled for
hours
and she did
too

...then i realised that
she
saw
all
that
i saw...........

street-fighting 52
cold hands harm
rupturous **heat**
and the ***fucks***

n ***cunts*** ~

scruffling bogside

\~all ways~
\an the **bowel** as/
*near*twisted under **blood**-n-**snot**-n-
fite ~ or ~ flite is

shite,

c h o i c e s
do not exist
[we agree then] here
hear the crowd **!?**

youcould***you***sing

still askin'

Dear Anne
The 'loathsome' Eliot died 53
today
without my finding time to
write and tell him
[as i'd promised]
that
our Land is not Waste
and we know
no Hollow Men
sorry about that...
but now lass,
you can read Chairman Mao 54
instead...

Part '4' LOVE AND WAR

an image for this century
a small and frightened girl child
denuded by napalm
bloody yankee
t h u g s
l i e
dis
pas
sio
nat
ely
a b o u t
hearts-and-minds

Armstrong walks
on the moon
on my telly
with my little one
toddling to the screen in her nappy
i think of
god and all that superstitious shite
being dea*d* now
...had long thought it
was all over... hopefully,
it is now...

55

whaling~~~~~~ 56
flagged death
and sea~bird chorus
screams
with steam hauled
ny \l/ on un bear able
as she stern-slipped inboard
and the heaviness
flensed at
an the **heat**shrouded
release
juxtaposed
in_**iced**_air

foot-eye-ball
sliding jokily
and not
!somuchthe**noise**!
~but i can hear the **distant drums** 57
Jim~
!orthethroatgripping**stench**!
but **black**~oiled ***bloodi***ness
slip-slop[p]ed
sea booted
and this… **a** calf…
lure for
the greater circling
family
an greater oilyness
an' the eye-on-the-deck
kicked fro
but see-ing
[und BradynHindley's aus dort; 58
unterhaltung Deutscher]

you***could***yousing

'68 was different
...in **Tivoli**
surrounded by Tom's
unfamiliar oils
and Susan's braids
the rivet - patched
wok and last
night's rice
Jewish Socialism with
a Brooklyn accent
and peculiarly
self-slant*ed*
which the Mexicans
at the garage
despised
totally and laughed
at when we
took the tube to 23rd street
for work
or when we drank *Tequila*
in Clancy's Bar
by Schoders's
book store in **the**
Village
Old New
York leaves tumbling
through a**utumn ai**r 59

'...au-tumn in New York
is often mingle-d with pain...
au-tumn in New York
it's good to live-it a-gain...'

and at dusk with
oil lamps
burning
writing poetry
for Tom's ballet scenes
~~~ a poster on 35th street
proclaims
'Fight of the Week!
Huey P Newton V *J* Edg*ar* Hoov*er*' 60
...Susan said 'the fight's rigged...'
Tom sucked on his corn-cob:-
'Hoover will employ his
feminine intuition...'
and i wrote
"...the dance is done
the singer sings
an armed man's
waiting in the wings..."
~those really were the days 61
Mary~
ALL **power** to the people 62
~~~

between slots
in the ad-verts
trendy *Vanessa* in her
Sunday-best 63
head-ban**d**
and Prince *Tariq*
in the shade of the
baldly brooding
feathered
fascist
scavenger
on its eyrie
above
the Ministry of
some-kind-of
Truth
posed for the
youth
and
Ho Ho Ho Chi Minh
Ho Ho Ho Chi Minh
Ho

ho ho ho ho...

a paper
tank attacked the Monday Clubbers
in Grosvenor Square.
Helmeted Durham miners
charged ... arms-linked
into horses and knight-sticks
into the valley of debt...
Geordie Cong ! Geordie Cong !

then home
to watch it on telly...
The Revolution
Live The Revolution
Long Live The Revolution...

Tommie and John 64
medals round their
black necks
black-gloved fists
raised high
above bowed heads
King
still moist in his
martyr's coffin ~~
social
revolution
not *asked* for
uncle tom;
de~man~ded

ronan shuffles 65
concrete cards
like concrete
poetry and
deals lop*sided*
beauty as tribute *to the dead*

Enoch told us 66
so it must be true
leering behind his
cockroach grin
he told **us** about
black men with
whip-hands
about
the Tiber
foaming with blood
menacing, grinning picaninnis
Nabarrow in a comic moustache
=a-music-hall-joke=
climbed
on the band-wagon to
the sickening sounds of
2000 dockers
marching
and Oxley Street
working-man's-club
re-asserted 'whites only'...
pictures of black-children
on the telly news
and tabloid editors carefully
selecting photos
and who to interview
Powell spoke Greek
read the classics
wrote 'intellectual' poetry
and spouted
ill – conceived
and **cowardly**
shite

who is

Reeth village threw
me back to memories
of all that i'd tried to
e s c a p e
how i wasted eight whole months
... the endless lonliness ...
dry-dyking in the
Yorkshire dales
is beyond me now

but at the end i lost
wife '2'
'the face'
and my s-a n i~t/y

The Face ~ the freshness
~ thunder rolled
across taut shoulders
crushing soaked celandines
and sweet-smelling wild thyme
fucking like
{only} sixteen year olds
can...
(The Crests betokened; '16 Candles. 67
make a loveleeeey light...'
and Charlie and Caril did
things their way
on the way to his fry-up) 68
we...
...should have let the thunders'

applause \\\ suffice but no...
~i gathered flowers constantly
and came each time you called~ 69
strutted naive
together|ness|
smothered lust with
children
deformed **love into**
r o u t i n e
until that night
while you sat in our
cr{d}amp\ed rooms

i made *flight* for
a different world and ~left~
you
to nourish a warmly simmering
h*atred*

...it was cowar...
with no concern for...
but maybe my...
saved the...
/though ultimately
naivety was the one cited\
[& 'under the spreading chestnut tree'
of juvenile llusovte
'i sold you and you sold me---'] 70

i spray--paint
FREE NELSON MANDELA
now
and live a different life
yet still i need your friendship...
your absolution...
but the decapitated photo\graphs

tell me that you feel still
only
anger
~...like the others
you knew me as
...the extremity...
both ends of humanity...~ 71
older i lay one brick on another
but know the gulf's too wide
to bridge
and the smouldering remnants
in a selective mind
permanently irritate my eyes
a concrete reminder
of another bridge *burnt*
a constant reminder
of a bitter sweetness
polluted by youth

life breaks where no life lay before
the seed multiplies
each single *beat* of Time
What lull and [void] awaits this infant?
What great **R**e**aper** claims you even now?
all that's passed,
all that's been,

is nothing
and my own ***past***;
a speck in **T**ime,
a droplet in the ***raging*** chaos,
as if it never was,

prepares for this ...n o t h i n g n e s s
...life beats where no Life lay
and all i feel is ***fear*** and ***pain***.

What vacuum a~waits you infant?
What light**less** void for you?
What trimmed and
sculptured
fragment of Eternity
has your name ***sc**raped* upon it?

the country side is quiet 72
the country park
is closed
red and white tape
barriers each canal-side
path and strollers
stroll
on tarmac roads
on concrete pavements
...beyond the tapes
silence simmers
a bead eyed
blackbird sings no
song but cocks her
head to listen to
the sound of a silence
that cuts the still
frosted air like
the ghosts of gunshots
and in this air
the smell of flesh
...burning...

Waterloo Road
nights ~ my
high rise flat; Tom
and Suzy exhibiting
their latest oils
reminding us
that if we
so wished it was now legal
for us to stuff dick into
male arse

~: }providing we don't
frighten the horses{ :~ [73]

Tram-Frank lapsing into
Russian
and reading Pravda

The Dealer
delivering poetry
exploding it through
the filter of his beard
"...after they have tired
of the brilliance of cities and..." [74]
...and
thus purified it lifted our hearts as
we passed around
the {u=n}holy Dimy***ril*** + [75]
burdock pop,
hirondelle wine
lysergic acid
and the long fat
j o i n t s

whilst <u>*my*</u> child
slept through it all
in <u>*my*</u> arms
and
Colin's
Chinese wife,

{slender as a pencil,
sexy in split silk,}

smiled as though
comprehending...

BUT

contemplating...
[loneliness
suicide]

whilst each of **us**
wrapped in **self**
spilt~~~laughter
mo*pp*ing it up
with absorbent
Comrade*ship*

while Che lies
cold in Bolivia [76]

Part '5' LEAVING HOME

leaving you
for the last time
cloaked in mist
there are **no** regrets
you hold **no** memories
of any import
beyond my 30th year
and these envelope
too many deaths
too much waste
too much of petty insignificance
it would make no difference
in the scheme of things
if the mist which shrouds you now
en***shroud***ed you for all time
buried you in the *h*el***l***
in which you smothered
so many of your own

in Liverpool
breath comes easier as i
wish upon you
only this
may you moulder alone
fade like a bad dream
from all memory
for you are surely
beyond redemption
oh land of bigotry and cant
perverse crucible of my
unfortunate b*i*rth

...and all that i could wish you

is

that

Cold bombs should rip the place apart
tear out the bowels, destroy the heart
consign hotels of sham facade
to rubble in a builders' yard.

From Calf of Man to Point of Ayre
infect the foul polluted air
with every virulent disease
and burn with fire the House of Keys.

Take Ramsey, hurl it in the sea
and Peel, St Judes and Regaby,
not a town is worth preserving
not a single soul deserving.

This land of bigotry and cant
where all the natives scream and rant
with viperous and intolerant voice,
obliterate; we have no choice...

then Mannin Line will not pollute
God's airwaves with the undilute
ravings of bitter twisted souls,
in Hell they should be, shovelling coals...

and children will no longer cower
in fear of blind abuse of power
which, with no conscience to be searched,
would have it that they should be birched...

and the old, whose faltering cries ignored
by tax-dodgers with wealth to hoard,
will suffer no more the indignity
of lives of toil, then poverty.

So send the bombs, release disease,
lay waste these wastrels in their ease,
destroy the bloody Isle of Man
eradicate it, **while you can**

not yet fully enrolled King Street 77
Commies **out**side on the
pavement ***picket***ing
in the
vinegar-riddled
rain and
Colonel John
Wayne **in**side shooting 78
gooks
and adjusting his green
beret above his
red neck~~~

~~~tired of the reactions we set
instead some corn-bait
and Terry and
i then (pigeon laden)
bought two tickets
to the Manchester Odeon
[the cheapest]
and Dai, **Dai** we
let the newly politicised
& thus beauti**ful**
pidgeons **fly**
high through the **s**m**oke**
r**i**ddl**e**d
p r o j e c t i o n b**e**a**m**s
to **shite** on
those **who thought**
it **gung ho** **to applaud**
yankee-fascism
~~~

...de**spite**

Charlie's family pressures 79
and the
helter-skelter
of blackbirds
singing at the break
of a blood-riddled dawn
over
Cielo Drive...

despite that

...in '69 80
we matured
a little
decided we'd *no* longer
s t r e t c h *the* necks
of murderers (?)
and an acceptable quota
of innocents
Hanratty, Smith,
Bentley, Ellis...
sleep easier
in your
lime-stained
graves
relive no more
in your
sleep of death
the horror
the cruelty
the unfeeling 'acceptability'
of
'occasional errors'

ironic though that
Jan should choose to offer up
his youth and life then
on a Prague street... 81

Leila alone 82
with your strength;

from where does it stem

Comrade

and the love they feel;

from where does it spring

...but later, in the eighties
when i **was** a token Scouse and
King Street approved
they decided
it was **a woman's right to**
choose
and, discovering that ***every***
male
chauvinist p i g
in our branch agreed,
i refused
and was suspended~~~~
in any case ~~~~~~~ 83
{Emmett's lover} had
died and her **blues**
passed on to me...

The 70's Match of the day;
final game of final set, official score card:

Soup Dragon
Carter
Hotlips Houlihan
MASH 4077

clogs an' flares
Nixon
Grease

15 Love

The Goodies
Bo Derek
Woodstock

Mork and Mindy
Farrah Fawcett

30 Love

Close Encounters
The Flying Circus
Radar O'Reilly
Kes; the Movie
Midnight Special
Brando

Star Wars
The Partridge Family
Stylophone
Jackson Five
The Waltons

40 Love

Janis Joplin
Red Robbo
Brazil
Ali
Let it be
Isle of Wight
Woody Allen

Wings
Liberace
Italy
Foreman
Baby Love
Mungo Jerry

Game, Set and Match;

}now into de-tox{

Part '6' HAZY DAYS

Dr Conroy's s p i d e r y
fingers
replaced the pen on **the desk** and closed the folder.

"Well now. You seem to be making some improvement
since we tried the Lithium. And doesn't it make all
the difference when you steer clear of alcohol now?"

The patient
raised himself **uneasily,**
shifting his weight from one side of his body to the other.
He'd **been over an hour sitting** there talking.
Just talking
about his past and his life **in general and although it was** undoubtedly
therapeutic to talk
and talk
about his **'self' he gained** the clear
impression that Dr Conroy heard only
what he wanted **to hear**.

"i still get those black depressions... **and the *t*ablets**
don't seem to
alter that."

"But isn't that because of the **drinking? The tab*l*ets wont work**
effectively
when you drink..."

...that's made
so many nights
so memorably
funny,
perforates my liver,
drains my energy and
money...

84

"So the alcohol causes the depressions?"

"Alcohol is a depressant. If you *stop*ped *drink*ing the quantity of
alcohol that you do... maybe if you cut it down to a pint or two a
night, then you'd give the tablets a chance to clear the depression."

Dr Conroy lifted the folder and selecting a space in the shelf above his
desk, he slotted it in.
It was a clear indication that the session had
concluded.
His patient rose

u *n* s t e a ***d*** i l y
from his chair

resting one hand on the desk as he did so. Conroy took his
elbow and assisted him;

"Is your back still giving you trouble there?"

"Yes. A bit."

The patient straightened **him/self**.

"Forty four years of age and a bloody physical and mental wreck...
still, the alcohol helps...
sorry..."

"Ah you're a terrible man now you are. **Don't you listen to** a word I say?"

His voice **was** authoritative but
there was a **smile on his lips.**

"**You** be staying away **from the demon** drink now,
and if you want **an anesthetic for the** back pain see **your GP**, he'll prescribe something which wont **rot**
your liver"
"Like paracetamol?"

"Mmmm. I take your point. But you were lucky...
it left you with no permanent damage. Make an **appointment to see** me again
in a fortnight.

"All right Doc. **And thanks.**"

In the corridor he
dot and carried
slowly towards reception.
Dr Conroy **overtook him on his** way to
the
waiting
room.

He made his new appointment **and stepped** outside onto the ramp **that led down** from the doors of the clinic to
the path which
ran through a lawn... **daffodils**

and then my
heart with pleasure
fills

85

were beginning to bloom. He looked at them and as he did **a weight on his shoulders shifted slightly and he shuddered. Warm fetid breath passed across one side of his face, breath that smelt of rotten fruit**

and sour apples, breath that had a physical substance which
clouded his vision robbing the grass of its greenness, turning the
daffodils to sienna stained cups. All colours dulled. He shrugged his
shoulders hard and felt the tiny little hooves grasping him firm
either side of his neck. Leaning
forward he wretched but his throat was dry and
his choking cough produced only
a thin bile
to **burn**
his lips.

He never **remembered walking through** the hospital grounds. Never recalled
standing in a **bus queue.**
He may have paid a fare but then again he may not have paid it...
who'd press the point?
Who'd demand anything of him,
bent double and smelling of
hospital waiting
rooms?
But he was sitting in the bus and he was cold.
The door at the front of the bus had been left slightly open and the icy January
wind seemed intent on **seeking him out.**
From the window he could see gray cars and gray people scurrying
through a heavy mist but suddenly colour returned; the deep burgundy
colour of a Threshers Wine Shop with its warm and welcoming yellow
lettering.
He lurched from his seat and grabbed the door of the bus.
"Hey! Hang on! Whatcha think yer doin'?"
But the door was open and his feet were scrambling across
the tarmac. He stretched out both arms and
waved them in an **effort to maintain** his balance **but** to no avail and with a
crash he collided **with *safety* railings and** cascaded **from them** to fall in a
heap in the road. **Through the lattice of the** railings he **could see**
feet
which turned towards **him.**
Heard voices above sounding
Shocked
and
Concerned.
He eased himself **onto one knee and** searched for his stick**, then,** rising with
an effort, he sort the gap **in the railings** and steered himself **to**wards the door
of the **Off Licence. The voice of**
the Pig
reminded him
that wine and whiskey
were his only
pleasures...

...are like poppies
spread, you seize
the flower, the
bloom is...

86

He walked the half mile or so to his home with the doubled carrier bags
hanging heavily at his side.

The plastic
cut into his hand.
He never lifted his head, not even when someone out there acknowledged him.

He was thinking about **Dr Conroy, about alcohol**, about the Black Pig which sat on his shoulder.

Alcohol **caused the** depression.

He was always being told that. Had been told it repeatedly repeatedly for over twenty years. Told it by **Ramamurthy, Clucas**, Rattray, Tunara, Sin**gh** and now by ***Conroy***. But if that were true then
why had the Pig been there when he was four years old?
He could clearly recall his elder sisters **taunting him, chasing** him about the dining room and up into the **bathr**oom shout**ing endlessly** that the Black Pig was there on his back. **Could they** actually **see** it?
He couldn't.

But he had felt its ***weight*** even then
and he'**d wriggle his way**
into the corner of the bathroom by the side of the toilet bowl and press **hard** against the cold tiles in an effort to dislodge it.
To crush it. All that he **could** do **was** push and twist and repeatedly scream

'No'

to his sisters who ban**ged** on the door and taunted him, to repeatedly scream

'No'

to the creature who'**d** chosen his tiny four **year**
old body to **live on**...
for ever.

this little **piggy**
stayed home

87

He fear**ed the B**lack Pig.

He feared its weight and its hooves which **fastened** on him,
he **fear**ed its snout which rested always on his left shoulder
above **his** deformed spi**ne** and
he feared its **breath which crushed the colours and**
suffocated him.
The Black Pig, which came to him when it chose.
The Black Pig, which sat for as long as it chose to.
The Black Pig, which talked to him incessantly about all the horrors of the world; about famine, death... evil. The Black Pig which could make vivid pictures appear in his head
pictures
of Abbey and Arnie drowning, struggling with their heavy sea boots pulling them down into the unholy greenness of the weed-strewn depths, white hands waving and eyes bulging, soundless mouths pleading... pictures of children sitting in their own shit, squatting in front of him, too

weak even to lift their hands to beg, eyes staring, accusing... pictures of women, friends, lovers,

l o s t.

He was entering the door of his flat.
Again he couldn't recall how he'd arrived there.
The door shut behind him.

~~~with the dithering
crack
of a ship
going on the rocks~~~

88

There were six one-litre
bottles of whiskey in the carrier bags.
He swept papers aside and laid the bottles in a row on the table at the side of his armchair. In the kitchen
he discarded his coat and shoes and rummaged amongst used crockery which filled a blue plastic bowl.
He rinsed a tumbler under the tap and returned to the front room. Dragging the Calor Gas Heater close
he lit it and sat down hunching over it to warm his hands, pushing his feet close until his socks began to steam.
He was entering into a depression. Just entering. The Pig was there right enough but
he hadn't said more than a few words. Hadn't tried to choke him. Hadn't begun to abuse. Hadn't yet turned its leering snout to his cheek and his lips whilst **its weight shifted and rolled in waves upon him and his hooves tightened on his neck...**

He tried hard to ignore both the drink and the Pig... although he knew that he was merely
playing for time. That either the Pig or the drink would settle within him sooner or later. He reached over and laid the brass clock on the mantle shelf on its face. He'd prefer to live without clocks, without time. He picked up his micro cassette and clicked it on.

play...

His own voice spoke: *What if there were no clocks? No...*

stop... pause... forward... play

... fire above stopped motionless in a static sky looking eternally at a motionless and one faced moon for ever? Would time then exist? There'd still be night of course but you'd have to seek it out... to travel in search of the darkness. Darkness? Night? Would Effy and Gilly and all of his scattered children continue to change or, without the movement of time, would they cease to age? Is time irrevocably involved with move~ment? Still objects, the motionless face of the Mona Liza, or the red Porsche 911 parked behind the plate glass window of the showroom window...

pause...
forward~play

...andles with marks on them, great creaking cogwheels grinding

rhythmically, smart digital Rolex watches on the wrists of wealthy... no... 'elegant'... people,
all, all would be redundant, would never have been necessary at any... Time.

stop
pause
forward
play

...toms lived in Time. Where did these construction blocks come from? Maybe they actually reproduced, were living things, maybe great stars were cesspits of erotica, palaces for orgasming atoms to copulate... 'to fuck' is better... and every few hours they ejaculate their offspring out into the Universe to find their own way to survive in the great... great? It grates...
cosmos until they cluster and huddle and form new
orgy-pits, new stars.

A shudder in the loins engenders... The broken wall, the burning roof... Agamemnon... dead... Being so caught up, so mastered by the brute...

89

And time also contributes to the relative size of things. A mountain is twenty five minutes high or a man can be, [like ME!] twelve seconds too short...

He hit the 'off' switch savagely.

"Another nights' drunken ramblings... what shallow...

Krapp:
Just been listening to that stupid bastard I took myself for

90

...what a waste of time recording it".

He lifted the clock and then **slammed it down** hard. Fifteen minutes passed /1 2 3 4 5 6 7 8 9 10 11 12 13 14.......................... 15\ **tiptoed slowly across his** mind.

Reaching for the first bottle he filled **the tumbler** to within an inch of the brim. He raised the glass.
He drank...

all nature trembled

91

The liquid burnt deep into his soul.

The Pig shifted uneasily and then secured itself more firmly **"You're alone... Who would chose to be *you*? Who**

would chose to be *with you*? I will
tell you of
horrors that..."

into the womb that bred them they return and howl and gnaw

92

Another glass of whiskey passed into his stomach so quickly that the fire never took hold on his throat at all. Then another followed.

And time,
despite the efforts of the Pig,
passed.

The Black Pig watched and waited and when he began to relax and to speak the words of old
songs
aloud

the Pig suddenly exhaled and began
to recite
a litany of the dead;

"Verdi (who joked 'til the end), Bill (with his three up-and-down doubles every Saturday), Anna (...asking 'why?'), Mother (who'd tried to kill the Pig), Abbey & Arnie (guttering, drowning), baby Jo (lying stilled in her cot on the day of her christening), 'Sticky' (who wrestled whales), Collette paracetamolised, Simmy (with his cowbelled hair), Gerry (smoking, coughing blood, shite stains on his pajamas)"

"No!"

He was on his feet so quickly that the table rocked and his glass spilt its contents on to the pa*pers* lying on the floor.

"No!"

Lurching aimlessly he struck at his left shoulder with his right fist and pulled his jumper over his head with his left hand tangling himself until he spun round in his pain, lurched again into the table and fell unceremoniously to the floor where he struggled and writhed with his back arching and his teeth clenching until the effects of the fit wore off and he lay on his side breathing
heavily, sobbing into the
stained and
dust

as of the un just also of the just

93

strewn
carpet

It was an effort to climb the stairs and in any case, hadn't they all told him that the pills wouldn't work if he was drinking? He fumbled open the door

of the medicine cabinet and swallowed two
with water...

Clonazepam,
an anticonvulsant,
must not be
taken with alcohol
and is
available only
as

an **easy** way...

Almost immediately he began to sweat profusely and he sat heavily on the toilet seat **and lowered** his head into his hands. **His head swam** and he felt as though he **wanted to** be violently ill but he knew that he couldn't. There was nothing inside **of** him. He was empty.

Empty except for the half litre of
whiskey that was eating him
alive with it's poison.

'I'm sick' he thought, 'Not a drunk, just sick.'

[aside]
If not I'll ne'er trust
medicine

94

Conroy of course believed in **God.**

He wore that pin of his with the heart and the crown on it.
The only Gods **that he knew** lived in a bottle or flas**hed their thighs in The Picket on Friday** nights.
Gods like Effy and Gilly who **could be bought and used**
without complications, without questions.
Gods with no great design and no **commitment,**
Gods who loved him and gave him **everything in** exchange for a
currency note.

He found himself sitting at the bottom of the stairs **with the bottle in his** hand which he drank from until it was **empty. Above the exterior door** that faced
him was a window

...little tent of **blue**

95

and it **was growing light now but when he crawled** to **the front** room he left the curtains closed. His legs would **barely support** him **and he** rolled on to his side in **front** of the still flickering gas fire and **tumbled into** a stupor of a sleep. **Liquid dribbled** from his mouth and as he relaxed his bladder opened and hot urine **soaked** him through.

On the fourth day

let there be lights
in the **firmament**
of the **heaven**

96

the **whiskey ran**
out.

He sat in his ar**mchair in the darkness and hoped** desperately that the time **indicated on the clock was not morning**
time for it told him only that it **was a quarter after**
nine.

He rolled **towards the window** and pulled back the edge of **one of the curtains. It was** dark. He almost wept with relief.
He allowed a

...puck of a
moue of a... 97

smile to
cross his lips.

In the kitchen he splashed cold water across his face and noticed as he did that the Pig had gone.

"Tell that to Conroy..."

He spoke aloud.

"So fucking **drink causes depression** does it??? **fucking** Irish tosspot!"

He conjured up the **image of** Conroy with his **cheerful grin**, his jug ears and his leprechaun of a nose. **He** began to
shadow **box, waving**

...**but drowning** 98

his hands to
beckon the **image on**.
"Come on yer bastard. Fight **yer fucker**, fight!"

He lowered his hands as Con**roy** disappeared, slowly, piece by
piece

until all that remained
was the
grin 99

and he **screwed up his eyes to**
search for him.

"Fuck."

He shook his head.

"Anyway... got to get some thing **to drink, something to ensure** that the Pig stays away."

He thought briefly of the injustice of it all. If he drank like this for much longer **he'd die... but on the** other hand if the
Pig could come and go as he pleased
with no **control...**
how could he save himself...

from the **fiends**
that plague thee
thus 100

To the left side of his throat he carried a deep scar where a razor had sliced the flesh and **cartilage such** was the force,
the terror with which **he'd hacked at the Pig less than**
a year ago

The hurried scamper to the off-licence, with head bowed and eyes fixed firmly on the green and slime-frosted pavement, was uneventful.

He never stumbled.
He never needed to support himself on passing walls and railings.
He ignored the cloying slime that was the air
he breathed.
He ignored the traffic sounds and the lights
of warm homes

...and only a six-
inch grip of the
racing earth...

101

No children mocked him.

He was back with the door secured firmly
behind him within twenty minutes.
Within the space of two hours the
contents of another
bottle were consumed.

The room
is
one of four.
A twelve by twelve box. Sheets of paper litter the floor, paper with writing, tight packed with words. Handwriting which is sometimes small and neat and at other times... creeping across the sheets of paper like drunken spiders.

Some **is** clearly poetry,

...there are only losers
After the games
i mislead you with
In the Days of **Wine**
and **Bruises...**

there **are**
letters,

...how could i have
left...
alone...
you... when
you were so...

prose **is** stapled in stained
and crumpled
sheafs...

Abbey and Arnie drowning,
struggling with their heavy
sea boots pulling them
down into the unholy
greenness; guttering,
choking...

The walls are decorated with **photographs pinned or sellotaped. Many are of** children... A woman in **profile standing on the edge of a beach smiling** at a blood-red sunset**... A salty old man in a sarwester hat looking like** the John West Salmon Man... A **stereo player in one corner and CD's** scattered on the floor near by... a single chair... **a single table... the gas fire**... a mantle shelf with the **clock**... his micro cassette... **paper**back books piled high in towers or fallen **and disheveled**, soiled with liq**uids** and dust...
...a walking stick of Row**an**
with a copper tip
and rams-horn handle...

and bottles...
empty bottles...

Now he lies on the floor and his body is shuddering with cold, with fear, **with** apprehension. His clothing is soiled. His skin is flushed and **his face** unshaven. His blood red, rheumy eyes are flickering open and shut **as he tries** in vain **to comprehend his**
situation.

Ten minutes pass.

-\ -\ -\ -\ -\ -\ -\ -\ -\ -\

He eases himself from the floor to the armchair. There is a single bottle on his table **with an inch of whiskey in it. He lifts the bottle**. He gazes at the amber liquid. **He upturns the bottle and the poison splashes to** the floor. The bottle is thrown at a pile of books **but it does not** break. It bounces back and lies still and lifeless at his feet. His **hand rises** and brushes his left shoulder tentatively. The smile that **crosses his lips** is a smile of triumph.
The smile of a victor.

In the kitchen he fries eggs,
four of them...

...check out that
PhD Adny...

He scoops them ravenously **from** the plate and wipes his lips after each mouthful. His head is **plunged into** the sink filled with cold water and he mops his face with a **T shirt**.

'Oh the wonder of it! The terrible, illogical, wonderful
wonder
of it!'

In the front room he pushes papers aside **with his foot until several clean** sheets appear. The radio on the stereo is switched on. Colour begins to return. The hardness of things emerges again. Sound descends:

#...when afar and asunder parted are those who are singing today,
then we look back and forgetfully wonder...#

His laughter erupts in the empty room and dust stirs.
A green biro is thrown on to the table.

He opens the curtains and blinks like an owl as the light
returns.

#...then it may be there will
often come o'er us...#

In his armchair he stretches and flexes his misshapen body,
lays a book on his lap with a sheet of paper on top and
begins to write.

Neatly...

but *shakily*...

he prints a title, a first draft -carefully- the
opening lines;

Part '1' PRELUDE

'...the **vanity** of life demands
a record of all that i am
and so a
beginning;

on a day of quiet gladness;
Mannin is calm, and veiled
in misty rain.

we approach
Ramsey bay seaward
enter between the twin stone...'

Part '7' CORRUPTED MEMORIES

and thus writing
kick started dead engi**n**es
{though eminently
seizure-prone}
Night **Bottles**
still
assist
frogmarching ideas
into rank upon
coldly docked forms
shadowing
adjerbs in from
rows serried
gasp-at-the-wonder-of-it
an sleep so soundly
in the perfume from Morocco
colours **rose** on-it
reflection through

speCtaCles
bridges = reality
an
Saint an Lee
Un*win***ds** ~ on paper
as broken-~~**choc olate**~~
riddling;
pangs
futilised worthily ? for **the cause**?

i **choose** to ask always;
what is to be done. 102

/youcouldyousing\

your small needle **dried** 103

my mouth, was
pain***ful***,
and then, nothing else was...
but you did assault me, trying to annul
that which i my**self**
was

and ... ***you*** succeed**ed** ...
being too b**l**i**n**d to see
that as my fron**tal** lobes ***d**a**n**ce*d in the heat
of your sanity-machine **[in]**
and i changed, becoming acceptable and
neat,
[put]
my **'self'** withered and died **[out]**

like the sc***reams*** from Castlereagh

This 'thing' my **friend**, that's hunkering in my brain,
the unlabelled pretender that he is,
is **your** child, you have succeeded again
raping an essence with
***electric kiss**es*

leaving only a mangled **straw dog**
a **clockwork orange** 104
in the **shell**
where once the

electric memory of sanity

lived

brick-laying early on
meant kinetic sleep bitten
nights wrapped

n k**no**tted
broods **flower** on
mortared cavity **b**etween
rustic b/**e**\aked **b**ricks
walls weep tie
ered snots of damp. **c**ool
click-knit-rhythm
blur r rush slurs s stuff
~ lump ~ ing ~
of smelling crushed
lime - diluted
ask no**toil**
winter**green**ed
ooze drippling ~ sweated
bitter lunch times
bloody tipped digits
fro*st* ripened
and steam crestles
hung **stingingly** over
piss slaked chilled blains
torn rough tipped fingers
frost-pained
youcould***yousing***

“Hey; you mad or
something?
Shut it!”
snarled
Cowboy Simmy
through his cowbell
littered
ringle**t**s...

later George told
me it was
because i sing to myself
always

i was alone *celeb**rat**ing* my
26th year...
a turning point...
Dee dniheb me
and the coming
meeting with Jen
not even **imag**/inable

drunk on cheap
whiskey
in my chilled Richmond
bedsit
haunched over a single
glowing electric
bar ~~~
contemplating death
~~~ i sang
sentimentally of
Kevin Barry 106
'til; shamed by the tears,
i realised this was the 50th
anniversary of his torture
and execution;

...to death walked softly smiling 107

i left that same night

drunkenly thumbing
on down and
through
Scotch Corner
leaving the Ugly Sisters
and their desirable room
to find
a
new life
~~~

s**cream**ing Saab halts
on a midnight promen**ade**
[‘Ringolevio’ in the glove box,
Grogan tunnelling
through my brain]
cavalcades assorted friends;
Nature Boy, Lucy Drools, High Pockets,
Hannah,

Suzy-slope, Vinny the Pope...
high on an idea
and **Jen-and-I** vaulting the sea-front wall
to fall further
[chipped teeth times two
was a lucky omen]
warm air but a fire still
stoked

and the vows of **love**
so reverently heartful
with the Pope himself
blessing us with salt **wat**er
and wine
then singing together
[as she took the ring {all}
Nature *trembled*]
and s**to**pping other cars to
tell them
in the warm darkness
of ***Ramsey*** Bay
when love begun
and ***pain*** lay **f a r** **a w a y...**

i remember
joining the CP with
Ken
treading the
spectre-haunted
carpetless stairs
above the Duke Street
shop proclaiming
Progressive **B**ooks
being
interviewed
by Secretary O'Hara and
Comrade Vollamere
(the Russian Doll)
i remember the smell of
dust
the inane questions
about
The Raggered
Trousered Philanthropists
[Bloody Sunday's
screams still 108
echoing]

Ulster-men cheered Carsoni's stand
They screamed "We will defend yer!"
And they murdered their own in Derry's streets
Whilst this Wop cried "No surrender!" 109

and that it caused no one to
even smile when i told them
it hadn't changed much
on the sites cept
bricks were selling better... 110
but meeting Terry, Carol,
Roy and Eugene... setting up
the Edge Hill Branch and
my first taste of victory at
Saltley 111
The
Communist Universities at the
LSE meeting Klugman, Gagarin, 112
Valentina, McGaghey,
Cornforth, Scargill...
~and every one had laughter
in their eyes~

and the real
s
sense of Communi t y, that

i
wa s the core of it all
~true~love~

divorce
when it came some twenty
years on

was as ***bitter***...
as Sacheen Littlefeather's
oscar-rejection speech 113
acceptance

laying | one brick | on another |
| i heard the | beginnings | of
rumour | but
couldn't | | believe
that Wilson's
Labour | | Government
would not free | | them
|later, | the |
same | | day
picketing in | Shrewsbury
| i smashed | hard |
into the | *face* of a |youthful
copper | releasing |
| the *frus*tration we all | felt
as Des and | Ricky | 114
| rotted | for
c o n s p i r a c y

when Allende
died on the steps of his 115
home
Jen and i had Dan and Kenny
over
in our Hampstead home... &
we reminisced about
skimming stones on the L**h**en
beach at the moustached seals'
heads
bobbing
far out
in the salt spume

but when it all went silent
between whiskeys Jen tried
to tell them about the horror
which possessed us;
Criminally Immoral Americans
and
a fucking telephone company
~~~murdering our comrade~~~

Kenny acquiesced
but to Dan it was alien
'Manx Crab' 116
was chiseled through
~~~his soul~~~

we showed him Socialism with our
love and comradeship
but he remained alone
as he always did

and as he is even nOw.

and you have to do
something Tommy
the blind-boy would say
he, who'd come at Christmas
across the sin-riddled City
with presents for my daughter
and an arsenal of jokes and puns
on his /their\\ *blind*ness
with chunks from his novel
wrapped in his mind
to read aloud about
the flight of the sparrow
and fresh juice-filled
oranges to share
and he was there
in the blood ~ and the
fear ~ and the
horse eyes rolling
and ~ the batons
raining in
Red Lion Square 117

and my fear was
for the our comrade
as i struggled and fell
and Carol too fingers
b/ro\ke/n before
the cowardly flurry
[Roy went *crazy* and dragged
a cop from his horse
kicking - screaming - punching]
...a young girl, scalped by
a careering hoof...

but we found the blind boy
and were celebrating over a
Chinese
when the News
came on the telly
and young Gately's face
turned the
sweet
corn soup
s o u r

***

it was my
thirtieth year to
heaven 118
Jen wrote
on the fly-leaf
of the Blake
volume
and six kisses
when our love was ripe
later i realised there
was one for
each year we
s p e n t

looking back what
a **fool** i was to
let her go
what a bumbling **jester**
and these **white-hairs** 119
have brought little
wisdom for the same
mistakes...
still happen

***

they shall not pass
we said
but they did
and in the sum of things was
it worth so high a price
for when a week later
we Comrades marched in silence
i met his mother
face drawn and pale
and the look she had
set me shivering in the
s t r u g g l i n g
sun light and i sang
The Internationalle
with unfathomable tears
intruding

London town ~ London town
everybody hanged their
heads on down...
120
sun didn't shine
in
the middle of the town...
good to get away from
Lon
don
town...

Jenny and Roy
held my hands in
Hyde Park...

...and Tommy died too
just a few months later with the
sparrow still an
un-wean-ed fledgling...
my youngest
~who still loved me then~
cried in her sleep
Jen
became an automaton...

and i...

i dreamt of
Kevin Gately's mother

top floor of the students' Union
on freedays in April
with Big Pat &
Spanish-Rodriguez squatting

in front of the biggest spliff
resting on his leather hat-brim
playing Mathew Passion
on flute
with the arched **sun**light

resting on his hazed eyes
and
Dave and i speeded-up
p i n g i n g the celluloid
table tennis balls
that m~e~a~s~u~r~e~d at
each spinning cra/~~ck
all the academia which
we'd set aside
to complete

some other day //
// then next day
the 30th
Jen waking me to show me
the single word on the
front page of
The Morning Star 121
VICTORY
and we drank cheap champagne
all day
and danced on
the rain drenched
Sheil Road
pavements that
evening
toasting the
morning-star
and Ho Chi Min
and singing...

We shall not ceeeease
from Mental Striiiiife
Nor shall our swooooords
sleep in our haaaaands 122

...and all the passers by
smiling...

t o l e r a n t **l y**

skeletons support
and protect our delicacy
so when the Khmer Rouge
left bleached
and empty skulls
and dis~harmonized bones
stacked on the
killing fields why weren't they
bought by the Tate to hang
alongside half-sheep
in formaldehyde &
labeled

PostModernist minimalist war
By
Pol Pot 123

today *George Ward* races horses
mixes with the set
whom he obviously reveres
a twenty first century whip-wielding 'Uncle Tom'
who raised his lucre
by sweating the blood
from his own kind
...instead of picketing at Grunwick 124
on all those winter days
and sullen summer evenings
we should have
liberated Jayaben
by putting
a bomb
under it
and Ward too
in memory of
recently murdered Baader 125

Part '8' EDUCATION

tea~ching
=
being a professional

reminding myself
that when i dug holes
or laid bricks
or backed cement
or shovelled coal
or wrestled whales
or poached salmon
or
......i wasn't = /

eleven years
with kids who
were ***interesting***
and adults whose
introverted
narrowness
bored
in tense····l···y
who crept from bed
to car to come reluctantly
to the slum
then scurried
home...
furtively...

and did i sell out
into the hands of
middle-class
morality or
like Doo*little* 126
was i trapped into it?

Jen said i merely
changed {at}tack

quarter-master Eugene
carried a
fat forty-five
pistol in his
belt and got
coded
messages from the Pope{ye)
over the *wireless*
at night
he'd squat behind his
hooked nose
in our Geneva flat
drinking tea
hugging the paraffin
fumes that
rose from our
heater;
late snow
falling coating
early crocuses
'If we make enough
fucking martyrs' **he'd say,**
'they wont be
fucking martyrs...'
he '***disappeared***' one
night
and no one
saw him
again
...ever

when Leo the Hat
who swaggered round Parly
Street
and came with us once
to Grunwick
got cancer in his dick
his wife Arcedia
wouldn't leave
him alone
cos it swelled to four
times
its
size
we thought he'd die smiling
...but he didn't...

d*is*turbing
autumn leaves
strewn
calf-deep in
Sefton Park and
sucking in scents
of bonfires and rotting
apples
then
holding hands in the
glass-house
warm><th
like toddy in the
s~now
those nuns watching
furtively
as we kissed
softly in the s*had*e
of an
evergreen
like our *love* was
t h e n

Uni days in the 'Why Not'
with Patrick and
would-be beat-poets with one
foot thrust forward
pounding on in a rhythmic stutter;
feet-forward, eyes-burning, in*tense* (ness)
clear (ly) <u>demon</u>-straight (ed)
Oh ho ho that un*shakes*pearian rag it goes
on and on and on and on;
"winkle-pickers, snow-flaked, beat-boogie-
bOOgie-men, sixties, seventies"
Oh Jack Kerouac please come
back
[you've a lot to answer for]
"skid-lids, real-**rock**, candy-babes
in pink f**roc**ks, brothel-creepers,
shoes-called-sneakers, bootlace ties...
blue-skies (?) Moon-in-June (?)
Lover's spoon (?)"
hand me the s/i\ck-bowl baby
if you will
i'm obviously ~~~ past it
well /over\
/ ^ \the hill

at the end of our three years
    Carol-Ann and i sat in 127
  the Eng/Phil common room:
        'I'll never for**g**et
        you...'
she said
        'And why is that?'
i enquired.
        'Cos yer always
        pickin' yer
        nose...'
  she said
[but then
  after what i'd said
  about her 'incestuous' poetry
                she would
                say that
                wouldn't she?
                The sherry-grubbing Cow!]

at Hampstead in our Garden
building an orn*amen*/tal **wall**

as a surprise for Jen
i remembered the day   i stuffed
                    it all;
the image came   so
               sudden
             so   clear
i felt again the iced-bite in my
fingers
saw again the
                    hedge**row** leaves
brittle as **emer*al*d**
                    g l a s s

and the bricks
so hard **frozen** we
threw petrol on them
to burn them ap-art and
the mortar
kept supple with anti-fre**eze**
but no anti-**fre**eze in me...

just a sick-pain in
the
gut
climbing down from the
scaffold i leaned against the
still green wall and wept...
pissed on my hands to
ease the iced pain
to start the blood f l...o....w
then
when i'd given in
sitting in the cement-hut
on a bag of portland
in front of the calor-gas
bottle thawing...
Orry burst in to explOde with
rage that i was sitting down in
'his time'
i hadn't the strength
to
deck him
but that was it;
i walked the five miles home
from Andreas
through
heavy snow with my
level under my arm...
canvass tool-bag on
my shoulder
...and became a maroon...
sort out my own private palenque 128
never again did i
lay one brick on another
for someone
else's profit

the much-loved Billy the Bastard died
of testicular cancer~~~~~~~~
at the funeral i got the giggles
when blear-eyed Simmy
kneeling on his pew muttered;
'if God has to give yer
cancer in the bollocks
yerd think he'd have
the decency ter stickem
on with velcro'
i could hear Billy
laughing too
but not God...

Empty~Arse
Tunara
{reluctant}
allowed a shudder
to ripple across
his slender middle-class
shoulders
but didn't actually
empty his
bowels
as we sat in
the Rail Union Offices
and Carol
suggested that we go to
the anti-racism
protest
at
Imperial Typewriters 129
'tooled up
with pick-axe handles...
and kick the shit
out of the N.F.
scum'

(but oh what fun we had)

Kim and i
would
bunk school and
Bea**no**
ride on the
Royal **I**ris
coffee in the
Planetarium
The Every**man**
at night
then a huge
Chin*ese*
with spring
rolls
and sweet & *sour*
everything every*thing*

in **liver**pool
... a derby-day

postpone the revolution
...allow Mountbatten to live 130
a while longer...
this potentially
another three-mile-island... 131
toffees against the reds
sticky-striped tooth-rotters
versus
embarrassing grown-men
)the antithesis of freedom here(
]here they buy and sell human flesh[
...before the crowds
=\\painted faces savagely blue or red//=

thick en
into tides of uneven filth
i accelerate............................
...................past the breeding
grounds for tribalism
past the NF sellers
past the shepherding bussies
coralling the vermin
channelling them into
pens
...these; the
lie-down with the herd
roll-on-your-back-
-for-the-queen
chanting
mindless
masses
who
are herded and divided to
shelter, wimpering,
in hero-worshipping
gangs of undiluted
blandness
~this is no**thing**ness
and to define **no**thing**ness** the
shrines to the *heroic* dead
and a statue to a *wastrel*
who believed ***this*** was more
important than life~
...later
...when all that remains is the
piss, shite, macdonalds-wrappers
and
litter

i hold my breath for the

moment it takes
to drive~~~
~~~past...
but still the murderous scent
of Heysall invades

/...when the ranting
of racists
has died

and the *struggle*
against
**inequality**
is won
and the people unsalt their eyes
...what shall we build here then
proddy Scouse?
...what flag shall we raise here then
catholic Evertonian?

My Mate Philly:

Born on a **Sunday**
Neglected on a **Monday**
Ignored on a **Tuesday**
Beaten on a **Wednesday**
Stole on a **Thursday**
A murderer on a **Friday**
Condemned on a **Saturday**
To be locked up for ever and ever and ever
on every other fucking Day

...'til he cut his throat...
~~~

Quaid-e-Awam 132
developed a nuclear bomb
so naturally
we ordered his
execution...
today...
Oh Bhutto do you
weep in heaven
at the hypocrisy?

an object accelerates at
32ft per second
every second until
it meets another object...
or it escapes...
so when Pete
made his
toil-blighted
frost-cursed journey
did he pass on the way
through the stages
of his youth
and did he wave to a
child on the quayside
kicking coal at the
gulls or laugh as we
picked glass from
his head after
The Peel Do...
did a voice from
his mining past
shout 'Fire in the hole!'

did Yucky
and Bulla
Cocka
and Denise
Snow White
and deaf
old Mac
Screaming Lord Sharp

and Pinky
and all his past shipmates
alive
and dead
in New York and New
Zealand
on the Med
and in the China Seas
reach out to him
as
he crashed to
his god-blessed senility...
as he made progress
from
this **Life** in Death
to that Death **in** **Life**

\Cannibal Farm/
\Animal farm/
was not easy
a council maisonette
on an estate where
the *an**im**als*
ruled
rat-run
tunnel-crossings...
a man with his |foot
|shot off
struggling to wriggle
away as
a black cab lurches onto
the green; faces
at the windows
laughing...
Maggie, Jo, Lisa...
names on the ceiling...
and Jade whose
Somalian voice
would trickle through
the letter-b/o\x at three
in the morning when she
finished whoring in Parly...

}coca leaves grow
on Jade's winder sill
oh man dey give me
sucha trill{

and Kimbo...
...the day after
shots zipped over her
head when they robbed the
post-office...
...alone in her room
working
on her escape plans...

'It's all been a waste Son'
she said,
'a fucking waste!'
and then she died

i chanced **'fuck-it'**
one day
in her presence
just-once
and received,
for my pains
a slap in the mouth.
'Don't you ever...'
she said,
accusingly,
as though i'd blasphemed
or had physically
abused her

but she lived her life,
drank guinness
by the bucket,
smoked

like a chimney,
defied
everyone by having we five
and telling no one who our
fathers were...
(that was
hard then)
**'I don't need
men'**
she said

and she didn't...
except,
obviously,
for sex

money came from
scivvying
for rich *real*
b**a**stards
and we ate well ~if infrequently~
feasting
on stolen pheasant and
repatriated wine...
but you know
she never swore
in my presence...
not until the day she died,
and then it was part of a lie...

anything BUT
a fucking waste Ma

anything BUT...

Jimmy left his fingers
in Spain
said; *it would have been a fair swop*

if we'd got Franco...

Jim's thumb
jutted
from a flabby palm
and his eyes would light up
if there was a
new hand
to shake
the revulsion
caused him to
lean forward on his stick
~another *fascist* gift~
and explode *like a grenade primed*
with
laughter
=== and... there has been
no compensation
for Jimmy

yet===

but you know ~ what i
remember most about The Red Star is;

Jimmy Allen 133

***laugh*ing**

that evil Bitch
thatcher murdered 134
Bobby Sands MP in May ~
when pink Blossom
danced wildly on the
black
playground-tarmac
Brittania waived the
rules again ~
but 100,000 followed
his coffin
and in Litherland
salt-needles
danced in my eyes~
as i sensed it was but
a preliminary skirmish...
toning the whore up... for
The Miners

when Chapman shot 135
Lennon i sat in my class-room
at Litherland High
mind ringing with
the inconsequential staff
room chatter and
spoke aloud as tear streams
burnt a path to my tongue
you were wrong Mclean
TODAY
the music
and
the revolution
died
\\\the kids looked
at each other
but said nothing///

a Socialist Pegasus
El Caballo 136
galloping down the track
head turned seeking
nonexistent
capitalist opposition
with his nine
foot stride devouring
the 800 meter track
and a brace of golds
for Fidel
for his people

small men with guns 137
are ignored by Brit soldiers
when it suits
and these
clockwork orange-men poured bullets into
the wee lass ~~~
for what?
for tearing up a few cobbles
for being a Catholic
for wanting her country free
for standing up against injustice
or
for just not being a two
red-faced
male
in a boWler hat
whatever; i just know that as they
spat their wrath at her
and even as the bullets
tore her flesh ~~~ Bernadette fought back ~~~

the night the riots began 138
we were in
Adam’s place; the old

Somali / downstairs dancing with
one eye ever open
for the minesweepers 139
Kev tugging at the Red braces

s t r e t c h e d over his vest

... his skinned head bobbin’
... Doc Martins leapin’

Do You Believe in Love? 140
asked Huey in a glass case
Kev’s head nodded
his agreement
singing with the Juke-Box music
enwrapping any woman
who came within
the compass
of his mile-wide smile
while in Parly above us
the sweetly scented petrol bombs piled

high

Part '9' LATE DEVELOPER

October 13

sinking into depression mean s

~~~~~~~~~~

*s**in** k*ing into de*pres*sion mean s
*s**in** k*ing into dep*ress*ion mean s
*s**in** k*ing into de*pr**ess*ion mean s
*s**in** k*ing into de*pres*sion mean s
*s**in** k**ing* into de*press*ion mean s
*s**in** k**ing* into de*press*ion mean s
*s**in** k**ing* into de*press*ion
mean s
sinking into
*black tr*eac*le* ~ ~ ~ ~ air which
no longer slips easily into lungs turned
to
rotting glue
mean*s* sinking
mean*s* sin*k*
mean*s*
sin
mean*s*
sin
mean*s* *sin*
sin
sin
sin
sin
sin
~~~~~~~~~~

'Budd wins 1500 metres!'

puny pawn of apartheid 141
with your six stone frame
gliding the tartan track
like an electric feather
and, late in the evening,
the Newsman smiling,
calling you 'Zola'
allowing relief to hisssssss
from the mouths of the
ignorant
chattering masses

*

'The public have an
insatiable
curiosity to know
everything,
except what is worth
knowing' 142

Wills, Taff and Woofy
changed my life in **'84** 143
Notts Miners
who moved into my home
while i moved in with
the inspirational
and loving Lyn
and *precocious* Max

daytimes driving lorries to
collection points asking
expressly
for nappies, sanitary ware
and food

...**end**less nights ~ debating
end**lessly** Scargill &
The Revolution

in a Notts NUM club,
when it all en***ded***,
Brian made a sombre speech

and i, unable to get drunk,
dabbed at my salt flood
self-consciously
- head bent -
staring in disbelief
as i watched my tears mingle
on the bloodstained

'Loyal-To-The-Last'

T-shirt that
the emotive and romantic
Casey had given me...

phone interrupts and irritates
then i tremble
two words coded
and a silent c**lick**
...in the car
i watch people;
if they knew...
then :~ horror
silently entering...
her private space
she at some
menial task
soft footfall on the carpets
taking her swiftly
silently entering...
her private space
binding ~ gagging
~ blindfolding her protests
then all heavy
in sweat like a steed
entering her rough***ly***
'til she screams...
for more...

afterwards
a joint
maybe
coffee and some
marmalade toast surely
then home 'til my sweet and wild
child calls again her
two words coded

for no reason a memory intrudes
after the funeral alone in her
flat fingering the photos
of Mum with a guitar and
that endless woodbine ash
perched precariously
slipping the blue-backed playing
cards through my fingers
waiting for the valuer from Chrystals
then dragging the sum
total of her life down those concrete stairs
building a pyre of
the **£372.00** that he'd
told me **her whole life**
was worth

and your warmth still glows around me
in the sweetness of the night
and your heart is still as
loving
and your fire still flares **bright**
and the coolness of your tongue
explores the moisture on my lips
and scented hair upon my neck
and s l o w l y
moving
hips...
so we'll stay together Jo-babe
though the first glow now has gone
though the fire burns spasmodic
though love is sore~ly won
and though the heart beats now more s l o w l y
and perhaps the end's in sight
we'll still continue loving
in the **dark**ness of the night

144

beCkoning metal
wist
burnt and t ed here

go~**ne** ~ my patron\
\ising ***pity***
molten....oncrete dr
ibb
les~
~
~

like frOth ***corrupt***ed
sputum
clouds of degenerat*ing* dust
m e **a** **n** d e r
over Dylan's hills i
inhale with trepidation
the Heart of an unseen Darkness
i
see **the** **Scream**
i
hear the {***fear***}
eyes blur {sadly} at *head*lines
blaming
an alien sy}stem
eyes blur [**pride**]
as lines of young men
sacrifice their thought-less fine**st**
to sho\/el a few seconds of hell
into *tawdry* sacks

i think of you
and i making lustful love
now when i **lie** with another
a thought-crime which does
not result in death
but which I**S**
Death
double-plus bad eh **My Love**

and when we meet again
in the place where there is
no **dark**ness 145
what co**u**nts is that we
didn't betray
each other...
did w**e**?

Mother left me only the
stick which she
had inheri**t**ed in her
turn from witch-**nicky**:
stem of **rowan**
goat's horn grip
and **copper** tipped
|||embracing fairies' dwellings
satan's hor**n**
and the witches' metal
earthing me to her
each time i take it up
Animal
Vegetable
Mineral
Power
Soothing me with
Her presence
Balming me with
Her love
too lightly
taken

who is it

Heralding the death of free 146
enterprise she
rolled ɹǝʌo on her side and
tossed souls into the unforgiving
wave[s] ***goodbye*** symbol**ism**
too tragic for such a thought
yet it intrudes...

thousands roared
in the night-time
chaos at Warrington... 147
telegraph-poles
fell sparking and then ignited
in the night

Jim fell too
going down under a flurry
of batons and shields...
when we
amassed to return
our coach of fifty
eight contained only we
six
the rest were
scattered throughout
the surrounding fields
or lay on hospital
floors alongside
uniformed cops

But Eddy Shah never
fe*ll*

curled steep s
t
a
i
r
s creep down to The Casablanca
basement

and the thick C*rush*
of **sweat** and ale and
Good Time George
in the biggest
........- h a t
laughing
as i tell him
of pleasure given with
his jazz
and **'H'** pushed
from Frog to Terry
(pro-Scouse ***s c r e e c h***
informs *Margo*x has
entered)
upst***air***s then
to nail a teen **wh**ore

for a quicky in the car
in a side-alley
off **elegant** Hope
street
with two cathedrals
bracketing the **sweetness**
of sin
and back home with Lyn
that night we went to paradise
by way of crack cocaine...
savored the
breast
on the River of Time...
later i felt the ticker twinge...
reminded myself that 100
years ago today...
close by...
Mathew Arnold's heart
gave out
in these same
Liverpool streets...

that night in the
Gas-works with Jim... 148
Eric Heffer
teased me about reading
The Morning Star
in the **Palace**
hugely twinkling and friendly
eyes
behind those pint-glass
specs and we
talked about the old days
on the sites; he
a chippie...
me
a brickie...
we talked about Gorbachev's
prediction and Nov 89 149
...when we
were leaving
to catch the **8.35**
at Euston he took
my arm and said
I may not meet you again
good luck Comrade

six we\eks late\r
hE **d-i-e-D**

and Jim observed; 'he was unny a fuckin' Trot...'

the blorgan nibbled only
near the
bottom step.
it had always been so
when [skinny childer] we jostled
to presume the advant***age*** and
Ramsey Harbour
opened her arms and embraced
many of us
in her salty baptism.

Big George and i,
summer in/\sanity and
a scoop or two in,
though grown men,
took off to
Irvine's fish-shop
and scrounged from
the tin bucket by the scales;
two speckled, bog-eyed,
gut-splattered
cod-heads

...and became childer again...

fighting for the best step
was just as exciting
in our thirtieth year
as it had been
two decades past...
nothing was lost
{though we wore shoes now,
protecting our feet from
murderous **haji-crabs**
and their green, snapping claws}
we broke back into the ***past***
that ***Summer,***
my friend and i...

now; another twenty years on,
visions of boyhood
compete with
the reality of childhood
long gone:
the **fragmented**
memory of a Summer
reenactment
is all the **fading** mind
recalls

here it is now on the telly everyone - scuds 150
skimming - Arabs bleeding - an 'are boys' zapping with smart bombs -
stormin normin strutting his fat through the desert storm - and at home
we recalled proudly how we'd slaughtered the Argies at goose-green
- but not how 'are boys' cut the ears for souvenirs eh? but hey; fuck
this the wogs are fightin back now and the israeli nazis are screaming
fer even more blood - when will they ever learn...

when will they ever...

Friday 12th February 1993 151
in these streets
in my streets
a child dies
then...
...later
consumed in the bonfire
of misery, shame and guilt
sadness bled into
lynch-mob mentality
and in the Courts
injustice
and without
a hatred and ignorance that
superceded the appalling
brutality of
the child's death
the act of sorrow
knowing not
how to cope
the act of murder
breeding deformedly
breeding probably
a greater evil

a sun-shrouded day in September
grave-yard gravel under foot
a yawning pit of unbiased clay
and a cold, hollow space in my gut
Chess pieces moving with
purpose
between marble stones of the dead
alone waiting *cold*ly *dispassion*ate
for our friend to be laid in his bed
Hooded rooks on an elm-pew
swaying
rocked by the wind's solemn breath
and we silent mourners share with
them
the precise *indifference* of **Death**

[Save us heavenly father...
...save **us**]

"Ashes to ashes..." intoned in the
stillness
[red clay clatters on brass-plaqued pine,]
salt tears scalding, focusing
s o f t l y
on our Comrades brief passage through
time;
Gerry the cynic, the collector,
the one-off,
labels reflecting and hinting... at what... ?
for they never revealed
his courage in suffering;
what you seen was the **total** of
all that you got...
so we'll remember the nights of shared
laughter,
hot tea in the mugs stained black,
the Bushmills sweetly sugared
and the aces **back**-to-**back**...
but the story-teller's left us
and we'll know his like no more
and only the memories linger
somewhere in the core...
so now, when the bar-warmth flickers,
and our home-bound pace is slow,
we'll remember his ever-open-door
when there's no place left to go

[after the funeral,
drunk, drugged and abusive,

i turned to Peter;
'...in the *sure* and *certain*
hope... ???
What the fuck's that all about
Catholic?'
...but he never explained]
stepping from the boat back home
Leah Betts winked at me from 152
a hoarding... telling
mE lies

...and all i produced was this
doggerel

...full of it
you know?
bouncing inside

as**if**a **c** **ed**
\ / \
oil **springgggg**

controls movement

a canteen table
and only wo**m**en there
pushing to the centre
announce lou**d**ly to no one
every one
'fucking middle- \
-class feminists'

determined to provoke
(and only P**a**m takes
up the challenge

but too too nicely ~~~

Pam who had

told me ***you*** were
Danger /o o\ us)

then i met your
eyes
sitting contrarily confident

above that dis
guised
seemingly [**in**]
secure **smile**

what i sought was **a**
'fuck you!'
and your eyes said it
but your lips didn't
you penetrated
~~~The Facade~~~
clocked the **sp**ring inside
but allowed it to roll
when you could
so easily
have ***clutch***ed the key
firmly
fucking up **the**
mechanism

~

a facist reaction
or an act of kind/\ness?
whatever
ey**e**s spoke louder than lips

so i tucked it away

nurturing a pleasant re-**action**

savouring a
possibility
of friendship with
a
soul
mate

no
never to sev er
the
bond
we share
'til death
do us

p~a~r~t {of which is}
suicide

simple pleasure

in a bottle

golden treasure

in a bottle

drink to me?
~only
with thine
Ayes~

i have to write a love poem
but i'd rather write a poem
that doesn't give
a fuck about love really
a lustier poem that
deals with sweat and
juices and purely
selfish sex

i have my 1000 words
to write before breakfast;
a sword hanging
over me
sweat and ink mix
on grubby fingers...
but i'd rather write a poem
that wriggles under your skirt
and sticks it's tongue
inside you

i have a need
to write words and
a need to have you
caress my dick
and i'm fucked if i can see
why words should
take precedence...
...or love

words are blocked and tense but
your thighs relax
as i caress them and
your legs and lips
open as i straddle
you and fumble with this
uncooperative zip...

above me
accusingly
a sheet of
paper on my wall says
'less is more'
so i'm going to write a
poem now which says
simply: *'love juice is lovelier*
than ink... erections are
mightier than the pen...'

looking back to the moment of
awareness
you were there...
And we followed you
And your bright-eyes dazzled us
And your freedom lulled us
And you arched invitingly
And you spread your thighs willingly
And you whispered seductively

"Come..."

satiated lovers
groaned deceptively
and i groped
and fum*bled*
unbelievingly

the salt of your breasts
blinded me
and the oil of your loins
guided me
i swelled and rolled,
bending to meet your plump lips
as you screamed to me

"Come..."

then your fetid breath,
alive with unborn horrors,
burrowed into my bile-filled throat
exchanging
death-for-life,
deceit-for-trust,
impotence-for-abundance
and callous laughter-
for-tears of tenderness...
afterwards,
we groaned severally,

The Bitch
...and i

over twenty years have passed and
although
love-has-followed- ***meaning***
less• • love

not a day goes by
without
thought of **you**

now my friends have forgotten
and your friends never knew
the years we **l{i}oved** together
and i accept that
for troubling you deeply
all i've inherited 153
is a breeze, a wind that touches now and then
and reminds me of what could have been...

last night i slept with another ~
sha-red little and
parted
when the dawn rolled in
like the end-credits of a **'B'** movie

today it's an anni***vers***ary
i sit in our garden
pen in hand,
reflective,
wondering
with no jealousy
who is your
bed-mate
now
i know that you still remember
~~~ and i can't forget
for to forget would mean it
never happened ~~~
just as i know we've parted
for ever
al**though**

we'll never be **apart**
...for each jingle jangle morning

i come following...
................you
~~~

Linda's song

R.I.P.

i've been told *_-and
i find this oddly hurtful-_*
that **i** am a **cunt**
[she told me] just me? the
personalised and individual me?
excluding all others until death us do
i can't argue... **[she said]**
i **am** a **cunt**
define ~ ite ~ ly
but not just any
old **cunt**
i'm
a cunt
specifically
...this
one here before
you
now r e e l i n g ~~~~~~
a slightly bewildered and bruised
cunt
do the sagging breasts remind him
of aging labia or what?
the fine facial feathers of
a pubescent pubic bush... or
is it
just a general
anger-invoked
insult?
it doesn't matter for
i am a **cunt**
and that's said now...
but let me tell you
that
this particular, personal, individualised
and battered **cunt**
still
loves him deeply...
~~~ rather
-in fact-
like any half-educated - educated limp **prick**
**should...**
Eh?
~~~

structurally speaking

old Barthe

fragmented text comrades

(fuc~~ked~~-up a bit)

Tore R ic ha s and L e v s a p a r t
\rd/ \i/

he'd sexually reflect
on the pleasures of text:-
{trousers down?
all alone?
in the **dark**?}

the cliché is
you taught me everything
but you simply

<u>d i d</u>

before you there was
ignorance
and self-doubt
before you
life had been like
a casual stroll on cob*b*led razors

before you i had n/ever li oved

so what insanity made

me rush to destr
\\uction

[for each man doesn't do that
killing thing Oscar] 154

but i <u>d i d</u>

it's twenty years

and not a day goes by•••
the midnight talks
in our teaming city or
walking up the Wrekin
with owls close calling...

making love in Delamere
while a mistle thrush sang
and i photographed
your face as you came
with me
hard inside you

provocatively you sit still
inside my mind
still i converse with you
like a Buddhist priest
whispering to an unhearing
Spirit

it's past the gut-aching
self reproaching stage
i just think back now
and try to learn from
the immense foolishness of
letting you go

but try as i might
on soft nights like this
when #...i'm alone
and so lonely...#
Blame/Fault/Pain
attacks like
a *demented* woodpecker
behind my eyes
chisselling and *rapping*
the *words*
the *reproache S*
the *echoe ~~~ S ~~~ eohce* eht
the lesson s
oh too *bitterly*
{too late}—ly
learnt

[...after such knowledge 155
what forgiveness... ?]

Coops

[best mate and loyal comrade]
storms
into my house
filled with
ill thoughts

2/3 times
weekly
going and coming
hither/thither
flicks his ash
steals my cigs
drinks my coffee
slams
the bog seat *down*

with venom

and annoys severely...
when he invites me to dinner
it's clear that it's a
favour
then i remember that

**he sold himself into
that ripe
middle-class morality
and has two daughters
who play piano...
and is appropriately
house-trained**
{and that's
true too}[156]

late Summer sunlight rippling
across Bluecoat coffee
and your eyes
bluer than crushed ***ice*** and
ten times older than
your smile...

hair like a hang↘ing garden
of gold and flame

within this haven
provocative and intrusive City
ech**o**es = se**o**hc**e**
be-come
welcome whisp**ers** and
whilst ***jazz*** notes distract my
mind
i
catch you
s t u d y i n g me

it's so easy
being with you
~~~~~~~~~~~all changes
because of one
hour in the company of
your laughter **borealis**
lighting up my life
schem <e> atic
like the mast - light
flicker of a night-
passing ship
on a cobbled sea...

a slice of peace
making an ordinary day
taste

sweeter
~~~~~~~~~~~

the sun's kiss sweeps the rug-sprung fields
and the river's **blush**...
the last detail heeded...
dipping
below the fringe of the world.
i invent words and think of you
and the way we ***were***
and i jot them with numb pencil on
splash*ed* paper
and then juggle them anew...
but as much as i write and **re**-write
i know why you left
+ it is only *cowar...*
that prevents the poetry forming...

curlews calls skim the wooden **b** ridg **e**
where we walked between quarrels
and i drink alone the **Lambrusco**
cooled in the ***sour*** beck.
*
*
*
*
*
*
i need you now
more than i **ever**/ did
...not a sun sets
but my thoughts
t
u
r
n to...
el fresco picnics on the days
between the increasing ***pain***,
and you reading Keats aloud and
pretending
to hate that *'loath*some' *Eliot.*
*
*
*
*
*
*
*
you've written to forgive me since
and each forgiveness sets hot shame
kindling my self loathing and contempt...
there is no relief

and too many tears have flown
=[under the bridge]=
since you packed your heart
and set your sights away from a love
that **glowed** and burnt in patches
and i realise too late my lost comrade
that there are only losers
after the games i mislead you with
in

the days of **wine** and ***bruises***

footnote:
just, whilst writing the
above,
i
had a vivid flash b-a-c-k
to Niram in 64
and Dee and i
in the sea
eating orange segments
dipped
in tequila...
swearing we'd
meet up again
one day
sweet ~ but fickle ~
and we never did ~
and i was so much
older then... 157

gambling: sweat rushed
meaning less urges
{z}
best pric/\ed
collared and
aces **back**ed an **black**
then building
towards
what may be an
end

banking favouritism
this side
of screen wires
protecting... **what**
?
youcouldyousing

your gift scented
with
strewn
with sensations

what happened to the dust gathered-in ...your skin
the dust *in*breathed

go walk~a~bout, enter **dream**time,
scatter it in the warm air

the close neSS

impress it with children laughing
absorb it ~ gather it ~ wrap it
in rafia envelopes
pad it with
home-pressed paper
smelling of you
you're here
like the...

soft as...

turtle tears on a moon-bathed beach

when shall we two meet
again

what happens to the blood gathered in your veins
skin cool faint odour
saying it
better than it is

we will make it happen you and i
for your thought
full
ness
and your kin{d}
create
fishers of men
and whatever will come
seems all
all right my newfound friend

over
imbibing
intoxicants:
sin is filled with the world
and **if a book's not worth burning**
it's not worth reading - the filled is
the world of **sin** & the ***asterisk*** of identity
is more relevant than any artful
formerly known
as
and the
mere raised asterisk
at the side of '**sin**'
warns us to
"be wary;

c h e c k e l s e w h e r e"

all about

all about

Part '10' THE BIRTH OF TRUTH

trailed and paraded through crowded 158
London streets
borne on a gun; green barrel pointing
accusingly
at the men who walk, heads bent, behind...
and the slavering ghouls and grovellors
push to catch a glimpse
of a rotting corpse in a box whilst the
radio observes an unwitting truth;

"The crowds are standing
thick on either side."

women outnumber men by
four to one;

false grief fills **false** painted
faces

false tears cascade from **false** painted
eyes

false platitudes warp **false** lips

as the canon barrel rises to hide
their faces for a moment...
"Must have a photo of the coffin..."
they arch eagerly forward

in life they loved the ***b***ones of her
now they gather to dev*our* her flesh...
these are the people who dragged
the Princes from their grief
to parade their priv(h)ate
moments before them
the cameras click...

**"A Princess; murdered by
the paparazzi.."**

and here they are again
blatant in their innocence
still raging against the news-men
in a manner Calaban
would well have understood

would they wonder if these two
young men despise them?

trained killers carry the coffin,
twelve apostles of Death
and Carnage,
men who, if told, would lay
land-mines to maim children...
scarlet tunics and
the remnants of slaughtered bears
accompany the Princess;
Military;
arms held stiff at their sides;
River-Dancers of Death...
the horse guard's **black** uni**forms**:
barred with **yellow** slats---
macabre skeletons,
...death incarnate

a tubby bespectacled
man in a dated beatle-jacket
wheezes his new song
for his newly dead love
{for Marilon Monroe is
yesterdays ^ Dead Woman}
and Elton comes now to bury
Diane... a more worthy
more \post/ modern victim of his
lyric...

and the 'new' boy Blair

...and Ashdown

...and Thatcher sing

"Holy holy holy, it's politic almighty..."

for hasn't **the *nice*** Mr Bliar
already proclaimed her
the People's Princess?

(or was it **his** Princess?)

and is there a coup upon the
House of Windsor being
tested in this Cathedral?
Di's brother proclaiming

"the coming of the House of Spencer..." ?

Phil the Greek grimaces and sc<u>he</u>mes
whilst Good Queen Liz, <u>for*e*man</u> of the firm,
shifts uncomfortably

makes a note to have this
raucus ranter...
...visited

but oh she gave her life to the poor!

(well at least a very small part of it)

and she raised wealth from we the masses
so her name was exalted!

(though she clung ferociously
to her own forty millions)

and she clutched the lepers
and shook hands with the AIDS victim!
and she bewailed the plight of
starving wai*f*s

[just prior
to leaving on her private jet
for lavish luxury in the sun...]

yes; the Princess is dead

i had thought
before she died
that she was
a parasite,
a false messiah, a rather silly woman
more ignorant than sinful...

and now she's dead i see her
just the same...
her *subjects* weeping because she's gone to
a better place
proclaim only

the blind **hypo**crisy

of

faith

switch time back
to half a life ago
and there i am in Adny's seat

heart-filled with
confident
go{o}dliness
and
the world
sitting there
like a personal possession
waiting only for others to see
it ~~~~~~~~ as he

does does
he know how much i envy the confidence
how much i despise the time
how much i support the stance

how much i ignore the
ignor - ance
and a p p l a u d
the
c
o
u
r
a
g
e

set them /up\ Adny

shy them from

their tight little cUps
and set them s p r a w l i n g
in heaps of crushed **and**
sugary dessi{c}[m]ated coco-guts
that's why you're given youth
and anyway [be lieve it]
that's what you're here
for
i know that truth;

forty years on

as his contribution
to the American
(wet) Dream
Clinton gets
his dick-licked
in the white-house
'read my lips'
all over again
and he 'did not
have sexual
relationships with
that woman'... honest injun
Monica!

provocatively **jools**
sky-d i v e d
into my life when
The Net
broke
she was hoping at
the time that
her 'chute wouldn't open
~~and one day
inevitably
it **wont**~~
but for now she visits me
a ghost in my machine
disturbing me with her
honesty
piercing my heart with her
past
an innocent
beaten into
submission
by experience
i have already said
~ goodbye
~ so-long
each June 2nd
she seeks the way
least trodden
and my heart breaks

later
when the date was past
Julia sent me **st**range words
to **ar**range
i wept as i set them down: [159]

"When they won't leave you alone

it means you need assistance.

Trying to detach yourself inside

so solitude will return...

...the only way forward is

to crawl deeper, run, hide, stay there

and **cry**

water is comfort *ing*

but this is degrad *ing*

humiliat *ing*

the strange fat lady

defiles my privacy...

i count the tiles

repeatedly ~~~ obsessively

i say "i am not here"

speak the words aloud

endlessly the monitors bleep

indicative of life

i live i breath i survive.

They told me to look

to witness

to accept...

but when the small box was

sealed

the vision was lost

~~~floating

devoid of gravity - face down - weightless -

eyes wide - pick your spot - focus –
~~~

wait for the ground

rush~~~~~~

paperweights hold down

the manifest

the record of the h-e-a-r-t-b-e-a-t-s

The soup is lumpy, congealed, unstirred, powdery,

eating is mechanical

and pointless

Carnations mixed?

... for my child?

It should have been love

in the mist, tiger **lilies**, snow

drops, winter **pansies**, hooch

grass,

...not advertising

blurbs for...

evaporated ***milk***.

There are sixty seven square yards of tiles

white

enamelled like teeth...

seven up and **three across** is cracked

filled with grout and the sign

reads

'personal belongings are the responsibility of the patient'

Humming in my head...

"Three little speckled frogs

sat on a speckled log,

eating the most delicious grub,

one jumped into the pool,

where it was nice and cool,
then there were only
two green frogs – Glub! Glub!"
When you're...
i remember you...
but only just...
Red is the tone of anger
fear icy white
muddy grief
necropsy mute
kisses on
tummy all
swollen.
Engorged breasts drip
without end
for who is there to feed...
wake up from sleep
and i will **promise** to nourish
snuggle up... caress.
Should i have carried the coffin?
i wanted to...
begged ~ pleaded
~ asked ~~ sobbed
~~~ went numb
~~~~~ gave in...
Who refused me?
Anger is burning,
it was my right,
my task;

'personal belongings are the responsibility of the patient'

Part '11' A PREDICTION, SOME TIDYING-UP

Final Headlines:
21st Century dating agency
makes appalling ***'error?'***
dot.com
set to meet
pulped-socialism
[dot will wear a red rose
pulp will carry a copy of
The Telegraph]

i warn YOU **to be very *wary*;**
for memory has no function
as truth
it shades and s*h*ifts
deceives even it~self

that memory so vivid
those arcane certainties
of yesterday
forgotten
never happened

memory manipulates self
as frequently as
self manipulates memory
shaping and creating
consciously
unconsciously
subconsciously

an insight once informed that
struggling with
the erratic melding of
memory and truth
is a battle lost at birth
and that anyway
concentrating too rigidly on truth
misses the point of existence
for there are three irrefutable rules
with regard to truth and memory
and i think
~but can never be certain~
that mankind has forgotten
all of them

a man i called father
~for a brief moment
in my life~
smoked a clay pipe
and chewed 'old rope'
which spittled
crackling on the
open fire
eyes grey as a
north sea *st*or***m***
never settled on me
and he went to his death
without us ever touching
or meaning anything
to one another
he was just there
and he came and went
with no word of
greeting or goodbye
except for once
when his own son drowned
and i saw salt in the crevices
that seared his face
like the salt grey of his hair
and the eyes dimmed briefly
in that brushed leather face
as a single finger, coarse
and brown like a ropes end,
brushed away what might
have been   a memory
or   an unstoppable tear

my personal Messiah
sleeps close to a park bench
makes sounds like a contented bee
smells like fresh turned earth
looks like a rag bundle
feels like sandpaper
tastes like rough tar
smiles at everyone
i see him often at the extremes of day
as he strides out in search of deeds to do
or catch him scurrying home to his cardboard
kennel by the leafless chestnut tree
in Derby Park… but when the sun is above us
or when darkness enshrouds us in the iced night
he is seen only by those in need or by his father
who tucks him up each night with a can of
Tennent's Super and a half eaten pasty
or, now and again, [as a special treat - which
usually happens round Christmas or Easter]
with a glass of hot brandy and a mince pie

dear dear brother of mine
who never was
but is
loved

i dreamt of you again last night;
high on a podium in a crowd-filled
hall i was talking of my life
now nearly over and the few regrets
that plagued me even at the end
...and i was thinking of you

then as only in dreams
a hand caressed my shoulder
and i turned to see my image
reflected before me
we embraced and the crowd surge
swelled our brotherly love

when i awoke today
to the milk float's rattle
on coldly frosted streets
and the translucent darkness
of a December dawn, i knew loneliness;
for the first time ever in this life

the truth is that it's all about vanity

Part '12' THIS IS THE WAY IT ENDS

...so the end of the millenium
~ **spent** ~
with Anne
setting off rockets
and doing a this-is
-your-life for me in her
back-garden in
Ormskirk
and later
while she sle***pt***
curled across me
recalling all the things
still to write about;

Alpha

knee trembler in the
gents' bog at Laxey with Effy the
Brothel-Bug near slicing
my dick off in my hurry to
force it past her elastic roll-ons
and Gilly the cock-sucker,
toting on a woodbine...
waiting her turn
and the birth of each child
bewildering me
grieving me at the loss
and the night in The Pool
getting split like a kipper by a sucker-punch
and blinded falling, stumbling

(hear the laughter echo through
the cottage window)

and Mum on a stone slab
and the cold air
kissing her hair so softly
~for she went too gentle~
as Kim watched *dry* - **eye**d

the force eleven
30 hour steam from the Bar
to Peel; screws spinning in the salt air
trying to break loose and send us all\
r
\d/**own**
stack-crashing
rivets-springing
heart-leaping
muscles-aching
sea-screaming

stokoe-heat
and ice-lashed-deck... and... fear...
or **playing tennis in the sunrise**
Mooragh Courts
then - still drunk -
swimming nude in the paddle pool
and when *the busies* stopped
in their paddy-wagon
offering them... but they backed down...
All the past which is private, unique, untrue, *corrupt, personal,*
Tebbit in his p**a**jamas in
the nighttime dust, trying to look Terry in the eye when he discovered that i knew Maggie's
sweetness, Auntie Scag cradling me - singing, give me five minutes more,
only five minutes more
only five minutes more in your arms...
Patrick and i in the Somali
in
our graduation gowns, Jo in a blue sailor's dre**s**s, swallowing bombers on a
Summer's night in Parly (take on the world man!), Uncle Jack carrying crippled Ruby,
Jellybabe smothered in rich warm cream: back curved to me like a swan's neck, the sweet thrill
as i pressed the gun into that dud-money-swopper's ear, **Jimmy** Reed on the Clyde,
Jimmy Rand in the furnaces, **Jimmy** Allen in the Red Star, **Jimmy** McGovern
debating, **Jimmy** Simmons laughing drunkenly in a tax**i**, **Jimmy** Ferguson going down
beneath a sea of blue serge, and... hardly knowing
Jimmy Corkish... and not knowing at all; my other lost
brother...
16th birthday in a detention centre, caught naked in the wardrobe in Antrim (*'it doesn't happen
like this in the Movies mister'*), **f**acing fascist Lord Lane, killing those kids near Kate's Cottage
(to be or not...), creating a Union and getting elected, hycockalorum and blindfold boxing,
Verdi in his bouncer suit refusing to bounce me, René and Avvy 16 & 14
snuggling either side in the Barn's brass-bed, Ski-man hanging
naked and lifeless from a light-flex, Tina kneeling smiling & knickerless in the gorse
patch by the swimming hole, first
acid-trip with Tom the Yank who
loaned me his soul to wear, 21st birthday in cell-18 Victoria
Road prison, (built with bricks of shame) scuba diving beneath the iron
pier, sucking morphine in the Royal as my gu**t** bust and bled dry,
facing the SPG for the first time with Kevin
(and bottling!),
the **h**eart-gutting moment when she =the only one=
walked
out,
decking that NF scumball in Preston ~ a single
punch smooth as a Stalinist promise, loyalist
clubs in Belfast being wary,
trying to k i l l F**r**ank with that hand-axe, [under orders]
stealing the communal jeep
at Niram, learning to sqeeeeeze
a trigger,
discovering oxygen blindness,
picnics in the r**o**asted hills above
the orange groves, the stolen
Humber Hawk filled with stolen

cigarettes, never fearing the
system - always fearing a size 12
boot
marveling at {and
horrified at} Chinese Whispers
aka
Democratic Centralism
?
Whatever <>
they led to
preferred lists
'preferred lists'
revealed in Gordon Smith's, {i
thought it was a joke}
sunshinecorner + the sally +
tambo**u**rines + hot sand, mother's
love (she should have died
hereafter...) pits wreathed with
bloodied feathers outside
Strathan,
knowing the clarity of it
all when watching Inherit the Wind
for
the fifth time in the Cinema ~
March & Tracey pointing to Damascus ~

bunking school to
shag that 14yr old under the
arches with scents
of licorice root and wild garlic -still with me-,
mending walls in the dales alone reciting
Robert Frost,
the cool and friendly feel of a
petrol bomb (the world's in a terrible state of chassis
Joxer),
Mave sterilizin**g**
cement-boat blisters, rock pools filled with crabs
and anemones,
loving (and pretending)
laug**h**ing (and crying)
demanding (and betraying)
working (and stealing)
or nothing nothing nothing at all

#They say that at the Vindi, the food is
very fine.. .#, *nothing*, #
I've gorra brotherrrr Syllllvest...# *gone*,
Lipstick on your collar told the tale on
yooooo # ***f**orgotten*, #
Hang down yer head Tom Dooly, poor boy yer
bound ter die... # *half-dreamt*, #

Sheeeee was oooonly sixteeeen, oo~~**000000**

only
.*# loving#*
Regrets, not just a few, far too
many, to even mention... *# no*
change there #

six *teeeen.......*

the f... the fut... the
futil... the
futilityyyyy,
but ohhhh the
pleasure too
yes the
pleasure,

memories...
{not} fade away
tooooo

Omega

anyway... before the third day

i will surely rise again.. as the dead do

(but **the dead**
move fast
zapping past
at a rate of knots
loose-limbed blurs
with serious faces
always just out of vision
unless you blink rapidly
until your eyelids hurt
with the effort
then you see them
ghostly outlines
with pale blur-streaks
dragging you into their
multi-curved wake
urging you to follow)

oh and thanks to whoever for the beautiful accident [and the fish]

...after death i think then i shall
become **Ghen**gis Khan and
Uncle Jo Sta**l**in
rolled into one
for there are
endless possibilities

then
i think we shall
enslave the scousers and
form them into
an anti-kulak league
and swoop upon the **Isle of**
Man to lay waste Laxey

or the Empire of the Yo Yo Indians...

Or
i might be a Neil *Kin*nock-io
and stick my cowardly
boot into *Militant*
stifling all right to reply...
as One does...

Or
i'll become an janitor at a
modern
University
somewhere on the Edge
and scour the web for
sub\
\vers e ive students

Or
i'll become a PhD in something so
obscure
that no one will ever dare
to question me about my ***poetics***

Or
i'll become a hacker
and hack into MI6 and steal
their **pornography**
(or just hack them)

\\for ***remember*** what was said in the beginning:

for fuck's sake
all just **is**//

don't read the notes

especially note: 161

...Or
i think that one day i might just be
me

and write a poem that i'm happy
with

(so... watch this

space everyone)

Essential Notes:

[1]The mass killer Reginald Christie began his series of murders in 1944 at his home in 10 Rillinton Place London.
[2]August 6th, 1945. Atomic bomb dropped on the city of Hiroshima.
[3]In 1947, the most publicised and best known of alleged 'alien' crashes happened close to Roswell Air Force Base.
[4]Popular music-hall song in the1940's; 'I have a brother, Sylvest/ He's got a row of forty medals on his chest/ It takes all the army and the navy/ To put the wind up Sylvest/ He's got an arm, like a leg, a lady's leg/ And *a punch that could sink a battleship...*etc.'
[5]Russian Hero won the Grand National at Aintree at 66/1 in 1949.
[6]Orson Welles' film; 'The Third Man' released in 1949.
[7]'spuggie'; a séance.
[8]T S Eliot's poem; 'The Waste Land'; Madame Sosostris' warning at L55: *'Fear death by water.'*
[9]There are many references to 'Abbey' throughout; Albert (or 'Abbey') Cottier was the author's step-brother who drowned, along with five other men, in an appalling accident in Ramsey Bay in the Isle of Man 7th March 1956. Also The Tempest; Act 1, Scene 2, Ariel's song: *'Those are pearls that were his eyes:* Nothing of him that doth fade But doth suffer a sea-change Into something rich and strange.'
[10]From; 'Contribution to the Critique of Hegel's Philosophy of Right' by Karl Marx; 'Religion is the sigh of the oppressed creature, the heart of a heartless world, and the soul of soulless conditions. It is *the opium of* the people.'
[11]See: Genesis: 38:09:10.
[12]From; 'Contribution to the Critique of Hegel's Philosophy of Right' by Karl Marx; 'Religion is the sigh of the oppressed creature, *the heart of a heartless world*, and the soul of soulless conditions. It is the opium of the people.'
[13]On June 25th 1950, more than 90,000 soldiers of the North Korean People's Army swept into South Korea, overrunning its lightly armed forces and driving quickly toward the undefended capital city of Seoul. A United Nations force, composed mainly of Americans, intervened on behalf of the Republic of Korea, and for more than three years fought a bloody war of containment.
[14]Freud: 'What is right is what you feel good after, what is wrong is what you feel bad after.'
[15]The four legs of the bed were placed in cans filled with paraffin to stop bugs crawling up and into the bed.
[16]The Christmas Goose; bought early and placed in the attic to be fed on scraps 'til it was fat enough for Christmas; the unfortunate bird often had its feet nailed to the floor to stop it exercising.
[17]'Tennessee Waltz' by Redd Stewart and Pee Wee King. Recorded by Patti Page for Mercury Records. Popular song from 1948.
[18]October 26th 1951 in New York Boxing Heavyweight clash in which Rocky Marciano KO'd Joe Louis knocking him right out of the ring.
[19]During the early 1950's at the time of Joseph McCarthy's Communist witch hunts, victims were all made to 'Take the Pledge', and answer the question: 'Are you now, or have you ever been, a member of the communist party?' The actor Zero Mostel was indicted as a 'communist' and blacklisted.
[20]The death of Russian Leader 'Uncle' Joseph Stalin (Josef Vissarionovich Djugashvili) in March 1953.
[21]The Coronation of Queen Elizabeth II in the Abbey Church of St. Peter, Westminster, on Tuesday, the second day of June, 1953.
[22]Ruth Ellis was hanged for murder on July 13th 1955.
[23]Manx Poet and Scholar T E Brown's poem 'Betsy Lee': '*That's the way with the kids, you*

know,/ **And the years do come and the years do go,/ And when you look back it's all like a puff,/ Happy and over and short enough.'**

[24]**From 21st September 1953 on Classic Sci Fi episodes of 'Journey into Space' were broadcast on BBC Radio.**

[25]**James Dean died in a car crash aged 24 on September 30th 1955.**

[26]**Arguably one of the signal events for the dissolution of the British Empire after the conclusion of the Second World War took place in 1956, in what is known in the West as the "Suez Crisis." Precipitated on July 26th 1956, when the Egyptian president, Gamal Abdel Nasser, nationalised the Suez Canal. The crisis was provoked by an American and British (Anthony Eden was the British Tory Prime Minister) decision not to finance the construction of the Aswan Dam, as they had promised.**

[27]**Pianist Liberace who sued the Daily Mirror over an article written in 1956 during his European tour. Written by William Connor, A.K.A. 'Cassandra', the section in italics is a quote from the article Cassandra wrote. After winning this case Liberace coined the famous phrase** 'I cried all the way to the bank!' **He denied his homosexuality under oath.**

[28]**The 1956 National uprising against Soviet dominance of Hungary.**

[29]**Lines from pop song; Diana, sung by Paul Anka in 1957: 'I'm so young and you're so old... *Oh, please, stay by me, Diana...'***

[30]**As young as 13 the author used to earn money harvesting turnips. A bitter job in the winter months pulling and docking (topping and tailing) turnips in open fields.**

[31]**The USSR launched Sputnik 1, the first satellite launched by man, on Oct. 4th 1957.**

[32] **Jack Kerouac's 'On the Road' published in 1957.**

[33]**In 1957; Perry Como's record of 'Magic Moments' was popular. PC also abbreviation for Politically Correct.**

[34]**Buddy Holly, the Big Bopper (real name; J. P. Richardson) and Ritchie Valens were killed when their 'plane crashed on February 3rd 1959.**

[35]**Around about age 16 the author was taught to tickle salmon and trout which could then be sold on to restaurants. The idea was to sooth the fish by stroking them gently then slip a wire loob round its tail or gill area and pull it out of the water. Strictly illegal of course.**

[36]**This seemingly implausible sentence was in fact handed out to the author when in his early teens…it was deemed appropriate punishment for a series of charges arising out of an affray in a dance hall. At his hearing the author was; fined, bound-over for three years, banned from Peel city in the Isle of Man for one year, curfewed to be indoors by nine o' clock for one year, given three months detention and six strokes of the birch.**

[37]**'Merchant of Venice' Act 4; Scene 1: "Portia: '*The quality of mercy is not strain'd*, It droppeth as the rain from heaven Upon the place beneath: it is twice blest; It blesseth him that gives and him that takes...'"**

[38]**From an early age the author earned money 'rabbiting' or 'lamping'. At night, two or three people with lurcher dogs and a powerful lamp would run down the hills dazzling rabbits with the lamp-beam. The rabbits were then seized by the dogs or 'knobbed' with a stick. One person would carry the lamp and the others would gather the rabbits which were then sold on to local butchers or from door to door. Highly illegal; punishable by imprisonment.**

[39]**When the harvest was gathered in the corn needed drying before it could be stacked. Huge furnaces were powered up and once started ran for 24 hrs a day as it was uneconomical to shut them off. The author did this back-breaking and exhausting work twice.**

[40]**Going 'on the beet' was common for unemployed people in the Isle of Man. Jobs gathering in the yearly sugar-beet crop paid well but the work was arduous and repetitive and frequently the labourers were housed in billets. Twice the author went to Kings Lynn in Norfolk and worked both times as a sack-stacker.**

[41]**Harold MacMillan who won the 1959 general election, using the slogan, "*You've never had it so good*", borrowed from an American campaign.**

[42]Cement backing was arguably the most arduous task on the docks. A cement boat loaded with up to 600 tons of cement had to be unloaded between tides. The paper sacks of cement weighed 112lbs each and were usually burning hot and the stackers needed to literally run up layer after layer of cement bags to pile them high in the warehouses. But the pay was good; the author frequently earned a weeks' wage for a single days' work 'backing'.
[43]Abebe Bikali winning the 1960 Olympic Marathon in Rome.
[44]October 28th 1962 The Cuban Missile crisis; United States Secretary of Defense Robert McNamara warned that if any Soviet ships enter the quarantine zone around Cuba they will be boarded.
[45]Lines from pop song; 'If You've Got to Make a Fool of Somebody', released in 1963 by Freddie and the Dreamers.
[46]On November the 22nd 1963, John ('Jack') Fitzgerald Kennedy, 35th President of the United States was murdered in Dallas (Texas). At the time the author was a 'fireman' on a coastal steam ship the SS Ben Maye.
[47]The author worked as a fireman/stoker on the coastal steam ship Ben Maye aged about 20.
[48]Now the term is used on the stock-exchange to indicate high action and reliable companies but originally 'Blue Chips' were the highest value chips on a poker table.
[49]On August 2nd 1876, as Wild Bill Hickok played poker a man named Jack McCall walked into a saloon in Deadwood, South Dakota. McCall pulled his pistol and fired a bullet into the back of Wild Bill's head at point-blank range. Wild Bill slumped over dead in his chair, dropping the cards to the floor and revealing the now famous dead man's hand; two pairs, black aces and eights... traditionally, superstitious poker players never play the hand.
[50]A back-breaking but highly paid job. Steam-boats with 600 tons of coal arrived about once a week in the Isle of Man and a select six men (known locally as The Big Six) would open the hold and dig the coal out into iron tubs which were winched to lorries waiting on the quayside. The worst part was the initial dig to hit the ceiling (the floor of the hold) and then it got slightly easier as coal could be scraped into the tilted tubs instead of having to be dug. The author was a member of The Big Six for little over a year. Vaseline was spread around the eyes to facilitate easier removal of the accumulated coal dust.
[51]Jazz pianist Thelonius Monk's 'Brilliant Corners'.
[52]In a small town on a small island there was little to do of an evening other than drink or/and fight. The author was involved in close to sixty affrays and incidents over a period from age 14 to age 21 for which he was variously fined, jailed, birched etc. This was not unusual; most people of the author's peer group had many convictions for fighting.
[53]The poet T S Eliot died January 4th 1965.
[54]'The Thoughts of Chairman Mao', published in 1965.
[55]Neil Armstrong's moon walk on July 20th 1969 ... and, at Wembley Stadium on July 30th 1966, England V Germany, the commentator Kenneth Wolstenholme made famous the phrase; "Some people are on the pitch; they think it's *all over ... it is now*, it's four!"
[56]What the author described as 'the most nauseating experience ever...' **He enrolled for a single six week trip on a factory ship serving four whaling killer-boats.** 'once was enough…'
[57]'Distant Drums' was a popular song from 1963 on; sung at one time by Jim Reeves. It was played continuously by one of the deck hands on the whaling factory ship which the author briefly worked on.
[58]Reference to Ian Brady and Myra Hindley who committed a spate of child-killing in the 1960's. Brady had a great admiration for Hitler and frequently spoke broken German to his partner.
[59]'Autumn in New York'; song by the Jazz singer Billie Holiday.
[60]The co-founder of the Black Panther Party was Huey P. Newton. J Edgar Hoover directed the FBI to put up a campaign to eliminate the Black Panther Party altogether, he also ordered the help of the local police department. Hoover, in 1968 stated that the Party was

'the greatest threat to the internal security of the US,' and he also pledged that the year of 1969 would be the last year of the Party's existence.

[61]'Those Were The Days'; a popular 60's song by Mary Hopkins.

[62]'All Power to the People'; the slogan of the Black Panther party.

[63]Sunday March 17th 1968 25,000 anti-Vietnam War protesters attempted to storm the American Embassy in London's Grosvenor Square.

[64]Tommie Smith and John Carlos stood on the Olympic platform in 1968 at Mexico City and gave a clenched fist Black-power salute.

[65]On May 16th 1968 Ronan Point tower block in Canning Town London collapsed following a gas explosion; 4 people were killed and 17 injured.

[66]April 1968; Enoch Powell MP made a speech in Birmingham urging 'encouragement to re-emigration'. When Edward Heath responded by throwing Powell out of the shadow cabinet, workers at London's West India Docks walked out in support of Powell and a much publicised working man's club reiterated loudly its 'whites-only' policy of segregation. What was not so widely reported in the press was that many dock-workers organised a counter walk-out against Powell's racist speech.

[67]Popular song from 1958; The Crests; 'Sixteen Candles'.

[68]In 1958, garbage-man Charlie Starkweather, accompanied by his teenage sweetheart Caril Ann Fugate, embarked upon a killing spree in the USA. Killing first Caril's disapproving father and then a succession of other victims he was eventually apprehended and executed in the electric chair.

[69]Pop song;' It Ain't Me Babe', by Bob Dylan: 'You say you're looking for someone Who'll pick you up each time you fall, To *gather flowers constantly and to come each time you call* **A love of your life and nothing more, But it ain't me, Babe...'**

[70]In George Orwell's novel, '1984', the central characters Julia and Winston, under torture, betray one another: "Something changed the music that trickled from the tele-screen. A cracked and jeering note, a yellow note, came into it. And then - perhaps it was not happening, perhaps it was only a memory taking on the semblance of sound - a voice was singing; 'Under the spreading chestnut tree ***I sold you and you sold me*** **-'".**

[71]'Timon of Athens'; Act 4, Scene 3: Apemantus: 'The middle of humanity thou never knewest, but ***the extremity of both ends.'***

[72]Foot and Mouth disease in the UK 1967/8

[73]1967 Homosexual acts between consenting adults in private was made legal.

[74]Poem by Stephen Spender; '***After they have tired of*** **the brilliance of Cities and striving for office...'.**

[75]Dimyril was a cough mixture containing drugs, opiates. The local chemist obviously knew why we were purchasing it for, with a huge grin on his face, he'd hold up a different sized bottle in each hand and enquire; '***What do you want lads? The four trip bottle or the eight?'***

[76]On October 9th 1967, Ernesto 'Che' Guevara was put to death by Bolivian soldiers, trained, equipped and guided by U.S. Green Beret and CIA operatives.

[77]King Street in London; the headquarters of The Communist Party of Britain.

[78]In 1968 John Wayne starred in and co-directed; 'The Green Berets', a film which glorified the exploits of the US Green Berets in Vietnam. The film was boycotted and picketed frequently by left-wing groups.

[79]Charles Manson's 'family' brutally, and with apparently no motive other than Manson proclaiming that the Beatles had sent him 'secret' messages in songs like 'Helter Skelter' and 'Blackbird', murdered several people including the then pregnant actress Sharon Tate, on Saturday 9th of August 1969 in Beverly Hills Los Angeles USA.

[80]In 1969 the death penalty which had been suspended for the past two years was finally repealed in the UK.

[81]Jan Palach committed suicide by burning himself alive in what was thought to be a protest against the Russian invasion of Czechoslovakia however on Radio Prague a commentator

stated; '*It was not so much in opposition to the Soviet occupation, but the demoralization which was setting in, that people were not only giving up, but giving in. And he wanted to stop that demoralization. I think the people in the street, the multitude of people in the street, silent, with sad eyes, serious faces, which when you looked at those people you understood that everyone understands, all the decent people who were on the verge of making compromises.*'

[82]In September 1970 four airliners bound for New York were hijacked by Palestinian guerrillas and blown up in desert outside Jordan's capital; Amman. More than 250 passengers were released after Britain agreed to free Palestinian prisoner *Leila* Khaled.

[83]Blues Singer Janice Joplin died in 1970, she was the one-time lover of Emmet Grogan author of cult novel; 'Ringolevio'.

[84]Lines from a poem by James Simmons entitled; 'To A Cigarette'.

[85]Lines from Wordsworth's 'Daffodils'.

[86]Lines from Robert Burns' poem; 'Tam O Shanter'.

[87]Lines from a children's nursery rhyme; 'This little piggy went to market, This little piggy stayed home...'

[88]Lines from Malcolm Lowry's novel; 'Lunar Caustic'.

[89]Lines from Yeats' poem; 'Leda and the Swan'.

[90]Lines from Beckett's play; 'Krapps Last Tape'.

[91]Lines from Milton's poem; 'Paradise Lost'.

[92]Lines from Milton's poem; 'Paradise Lost'.

[93]Lines from Arthur Clough's poem; 'Easter Day'.

[94]'King Lear'; Act 5, Scene 3; 'Goneril: *[Aside]* If not, I'll ne'er trust medicine.'

[95]Lines from Wilde's poem; 'The Ballad of Reading Jail'.

[96]Genesis 1:14

[97]Lines from poem by Ric Lee. (thanks Ric)

[98]Lines from Stevie Smith's poem; 'Not Waving But Drowning'.

[99]Lines from Lewis Carrol's 'Alice in Wonderland'.

[100]Lines from Coleridge's poem; 'Rhyme of the Ancient Mariner'.

[101]Lines from Louis MacNeice' poem; 'Birmingham'.

[102]A pamphlet by Vladimir Illyich Lenin published in 1902 was entitled; 'What is to be Done?'

[103]Between 1968 and 1969 the author received over twenty ECT (Electro Convulsive Therapy) 'treatments' in an attempt to 'cure' his manic-depression.

[104]Burgess' novel; 'A Clockwork Orange' was made into a film in 1971 and the film 'Straw Dogs' was also released in the same year (Dustin Hoffman and Susan George).

[105]The author is a time-served Mason (bricklayer, stone-worker, tiler, plasterer etc; all things to do with stone and bricks). Winter Green was a lump of sweet smelling balm which was rubbed into the hands to prevent chilblains in frosty conditions... if Winter Green was not available, pissing on the hands was thought to have the same effect.

[106]In November 1920 the British in Ireland tortured and then executed an eighteen year old medical student, Kevin Barry, who was also a Republican volunteer.

[107]Lines from a song written to commemorate the death of Kevin Barry: 'For the cause he proudly cherished This sad parting had to be... Then *to death walked softly smiling* That old Ireland might be free!'

[108]Sunday January 30th 1972 On January 30th 1972, soldiers from the British Army's 1st Parachute Regiment opened fire on unarmed and peaceful civilian demonstrators in the Bogside, Derry, Ireland, near the Rossville flats, murdering thirteen innocent people.

[109]Lord Carson was leader of the Irish Unionist Party and helped to form the 36th Ulster Division. He was also involved in the War Cabinet and formed the slogan; 'No Surrender'. When working in Belfast the author wrote this short poem to point out the irony that racist Orange Men did not want 'foreigners' in their country and repeated Carson's slogan unaware that he himself was of Italian descent.

[110]Carl Andre's; 'Equivalent VIII', alleged 'minimalist art' and better known as the 'Tate

bricks', was a 'sculpture' consisting of 120 fire bricks (arranged into two layers to give the work 'greater mass' according to the guide). It was purchased by the Tate in 1972.

[111]The struggle in 1972 to close the Saltley coke depot during a dispute between the Miners and the Government, ended when the police ordered the depot to be closed down when faced with tens of thousands of workers who had marched out of their factories in the Birmingham area and the thousands of others from all over Britain had blocked roads into Birmingham as they converged on Saltley Coke Depot. To have continued the struggle to keep open the Coke Depot, the police would have turned parts of Birmingham into a battle zone. Scargill said afterwards: 'The miners didn't close Saltley, the working class closed Saltley.'

[112]Writer and Philosopher James Klugman, Major Yuri Gagarin Russian Cosmonaut, Colonel-Engineer Valentina Vladimirovna Tereshkova Russian Cosmonaut, Scottish miners' leader Mick McGahey, writer and philosopher Maurice Cornforth and NUM Leader Arthur Scargill. The Communist University of London was organised in the late 60's and 70's and the author attended frequently.

[113]During the last week of February 1972 native Americans occupied the site of the Battle of Wounded Knee and exchanged rifle fire with Federal troops. They demanded changes in life on the Pine Ridge Reservation. Sacheen Littlefeather turned up at the Oscar ceremonies to refuse acceptance, on behalf of Marlon Brando, of an Oscar for the actor's role in 'The Godfather'. The speech she delivered was a protest against the stand-off between native Americans and federal troops and at the way native Americans were portrayed in films.

[114]1972 Building workers Des Warren and Ricky Thomlinson were jailed for 'conspiracy'. The author was a building worker at the time and drove to Shrewsbury to join the mass protests/pickets.

[115]September 11th 1973 Marxist President Salvador Allende murdered in a coup d'état led by the Fascist General Augusto Pinochet.

[116]The Manx people are fond of repeating a shameful story which reveals much about the obnoxious Manx character; *"A Manx man is walking on the quayside with a sack over his shoulder filled with crabs. A visitor stops and asks if the man is not worried that the crabs will climb out. The Manx man replies; 'No danger of that, these are Manx crabs, if one tries to get to the top then the others will drag him down again.'"*

[117]On Saturday June 15th 1974 the National Front called a march through the West End of London under the banner 'Send Them Back'. The Council of Liberation called for a counter demonstration. A young student, Kevin Gately, died in clashes with the police. The author and his friends were with the International Marxist Group. A female friend of the author's was quite seriously injured.

[118]Lines from Dylan Thomas' poem; 'Poem in October'; '*It was my thirtieth year to heaven* Woke to my hearing from harbour and neighbour wood And the mussel pooled and the heron Priested shore...'

[119]'King Henry IV'; Act v, Scene v; Henry speaks to Falstaff: 'I know thee not, old man: fall to thy prayers; How ill *white hairs* become a *fool* and *jester*!'

[120]Parody of lines from Bob Dylan's; 'Oxford Town'.

[121]The Vietnam War ended on the last day of April 1975 and the single word 'VICTORY' occupied the front page of the Communist Party's newspaper 'The Morning Star'.

[122]Recalled lines from William Blake's poem; 'Jerusalem'; 'I will not cease from Mental Fight,/ Nor shall my sword sleep in my hand? Til we have built Jerusalem/ In England's green & pleasant land'

[123]On April 17th 1975 the Khmer Rouge, a communist guerrilla group led by Pol Pot, took power in Phnom Penh, the capital of Cambodia. They forced all city dwellers into the countryside and to labor camps. During their rule, it is estimated that 2 million Cambodians died by starvation, torture or execution.

[124]In 1976/7 at Grunwick, thousands of Trades Unionists picketed George Ward's film processing plant every single day. The author regularly attended the Monday morning

pickets driving to London from Liverpool with other CP members. On 7th November 1977 a pitched battle took place on the streets of North London between the police and the pickets; the force of pressure caused a wall to collapse injuring several police and pickets including the author. The strike arose when Indo-Pakistani workers protested against racism in the workplace and oppressive labour conditions. Sixty percent of the strikers were women, most of them Gujaratis from East Africa, who went daily to the picket line despite pressure from their husbands and fathers to discourage them. The diminutive form of their militant leader, Jayaben Desai, was a familiar image in the media coverage of the event. She revealed the attempts of the managing director, George Ward, who was Anglo-Indian, to shame the striking women into returning to work.

[125]Andreas Baader was one of the two namesakes of the Baader-Meinhof Gang. On October 17th/18th 1977 Baader *allegedly* committed suicide in his cell whilst in separate cells members of the gang also took their own lives.

[126]G B Shaw's play 'Pygmalion', act V; Doolittle: 'Done to me! Ruined me. Destroyed my happiness. Tied me up and delivered me *into the hands of middle class morality.*'

[127]The *acclaimed* poet Carol Ann Duffy who attended Liverpool University with the author.

[128]A 'maroon,' was a runaway slave who slipped off the plantation to the free jungle communities known as 'palenques.'

[129]Indo-Pakistani women joined their men in protesting racism in the workplace and oppressive labor conditions in the Imperial Typewriters strike of 1974 in Leicester, the National Front gave support to the white shop-stewards at the plant who were on strike and several mass pickets resulted in confrontations.

[130]Earl Mountbatten killed by the IRA August 27th 1979.

[131]28th March 1979 a Uranium Water reactor came close to causing the worlds' most devastating nuclear accident ever at Three Mile Island in America.

[132]Bhutto, leader of the Pakistan People's Party, was executed following a show-trial on 4th April 1979. He was known as Quaid-e-Awam (Leader of the Masses).

[133]The late and courageous Jimmy Allen of Liverpool was a veteran of the Spanish Civil War wherein he fought with the International Brigades and was severely wounded. R.I.P. Comrade.

[134]At 1:17 a.m. on May 5th 1980 after 66 days without food, MP Bobby Sands died aged 27. He had been an MP for 26 days. Margaret Thatcher was PM at the time.

[135]December 8th 1980 John Lennon was shot dead in New York by Mark Chapman, to whom he had given an autograph just hours earlier.

[136]Cuban Alberto Juantorena (nicknamed El Caballo; (The Horse) in the 1976 Olympic Games won both the 400 and 800 metres, most track experts considered this to be the most difficult of all doubles. He dedicated his wins to Fidel and to his people.

[137]In December 1980, Loyalists struck against independent socialist Bernadette Devlin McAlisky, an attack which she barely survived, leaving her and her husband Michael both seriously wounded. That the Loyalist attack on McAlisky was able to take place while British soldiers were posted virtually across the street from her home testified to the blood on Britain's hands in the Loyalist violence. This was the 'shoot-to-kill' policy that John Stalker was delegated to investigate.

[138]The Toxteth riots of 1981 when the author was actually living on Upper Parliament Street. Also *'the night the riots began'* is a refrain from Tracy Chapman's song; 'Back Streets of America'. The famous Somali Club on Upper Parliament Street in Liverpool 8 was run by a huge Samalian called Adam who bounced unwelcome visitors/ customers with an axe.

[139]'Minesweepers'; colloquial; people who go to clubs and pubs with no money and 'minesweep' (i.e.; 'steal') other people's drinks.

[140]'Do You Believe In Love' was a song by Huey Lewis and the News, which was popular in the early 1980's.

[141] Zola Budd; controversial South African runner. This prompted by a headline on 'Ceefax'

on 29th May 1984.

[142]Oscar Wilde.

[143]The British Miners' Strike 1984-85. The author picketed daily and drove goods from collection points to Mining communities.

[144]Accident at Nuclear Plant; Chernobyl Unit 4 - on 26th April 1986.

[145]A refrain throughout George Orwell's novel; '1984'; 'We shall meet in the place where there is no darkness...'

[146]March 1987 the roll- on/roll-off passenger ferry Herald of Free Enterprise capsized and sank shortly after leaving Zeebrugge in Belgium. The accident resulted in the deaths of 193 passengers and crew members.

[147]In the now-Cheshire town of Warrington, in 1986, Eddy Shah tried to produce a local newspaper with new technology but without the union's involvement. Union's picketed daily and mass rioting occurred. Shah failed but he went on to use that experience for the launch of a new national paper, Today (now closed), whose ownership was eventually transferred to press baron Rupert Murdoch's News International.

[148]'Gas works' nickname given to the members' bar in the Houses of Parliament.

[149]Gorbachev visiting West Germany on 10th June 1989 said of Berlin Wall 'Nothing is eternal in this world'... on November 8th the wall opened.

[150]Operation Desert Storm in January 1991. US Army General H. (storming) Norman Schwarzkopf. In the early hours of 18th January, the nature of the war fundamentally changed when Iraq fired eight Scuds at Israel.

[151]Two ten year old children; Jon Venables and Robert Thomson, kidnapped and killed 2yr old James Bulger in Bootle Merseyside on 12th February 1993. Subsequently Britain was found guilty by the Court of Human Rights for breaching the Human Rights of the ten year old children who were found guilty of murder and sentenced initially to 8 yrs jail. Outside the Court rooms on the day of the initial Hearings at South Sefton Magistrates Court the author witnessed yob mentality as groups of thugs chanted, football style; '*Hang the bastards, hang the bastards.*' Several arrests were made.

[152]Leah Betts died in Nov 1995 after taking an ecstasy ('E') tablet at her 18th birthday party. Her funeral was filmed and posters displayed her face as part of an anti-drugs campaign. At her inquest however the doctors who treated her said that "water intoxication", and not an allergic reaction to the drug, was the cause of death.

[153]'Proverbs' (the wisdom of Solomon) 11:29 'He that troubleth his own house shall inherit the wind.'

[154]Oscar Wilde's poem;' The Ballad of Reading Jail'; 'For each man kills the thing he loves...'

[155]Lines from the poem; 'Gerontion' by T S Eliot: *'After such knowledge, what forgiveness?* Think how History has many cunning passages, contrived corridors And issues, deceives with whispering ambitions, Guides us by vanities...'

[156]'King Lear'; Act 5, Scene 2: 'Edgar: What, in *ill thoughts* again? Men must endure Their *going* , even as their *coming hither*; *Ripe*ness is all: come on. /Gloucester: *And that's true too.*'

[157]Song by Bob Dylan released in 1964; 'My Back Pages'; 'We'll meet on edges, soon,' said I, Proud 'neath heated brow. Ah, *but I was so much older then*, 'm younger than that now.

[158]Princess Diana died in a car crash on August 31st 1997.

[159]The words about the loss of children which follow were written by Julia Strong and merely set into fragmented text by the author.

[160]Dylan Thomas' poem; 'Do not go gentle into that good night, Old age should burn and rave at close of day; Rage, rage against the dying of the light.' The author's mother died very peacefully following a stroke.

[161]Please note that all the essential notes mean nothing at all... (except essentially)